Programmed Poker

Programmed Poker

The Inside System for Winning

by Jim Glenn

The Rutledge Press
New York, New York

Designer: Liney Li
Editor: Jay Hyams

Published by The Rutledge Press, A Division of
W. H. Smith Publishers Inc., 112 Madison Avenue,
New York, New York 10016

First Printing 1981.
Printed in the United States of America.

Library of Congress Cataloging in Publication Data

Glenn, Jim.
  Programmed poker.

  1. Poker—Programmed instruction. I. Title.
GV1251.G54   795.41′2′02854   81-5198
ISBN 0-8317-7152-6   AACR2

To W. L. S.,
an unstinting patron of the game,
in gratitude.

contents

appendices   131

introduction

There is such a thing as luck, and even a fool may win at poker, but it is possible to be neither lucky nor a fool and still win. Success at poker rests on a threefold foundation—the cards, the odds, and "psychology."

Methods for regulating the quality of your cards are either dangerous (stacking or marking a deck) or inadequate (hoping, wishing, praying). The bare and humbling fact is that the cards are beyond influence, completely arbitrary and completely just in carrying forward the law of chance.

What remains to the poker player is an opportunity to refine his expectations mathematically and to deceive and confound his opponents. This book concerns itself with the essential probabilities in four basic poker forms and with strategies consistent with the odds. The psychology of the game is so much a function of experience (for which there is no substitute) and personal style that only the most important factors can be sketched here.

A working knowledge of the correct poker odds may not, of itself, win you much money when you're up against good players, but it won't cost you anything either, and most of the time, thank God, you'll play against an assortment of weak to fair gamblers.

The odds are not exactly revelatory in nature; they are no secret. Most players have seen the same numbers you have, and most players willfully forget or disregard them with gratifying frequency. This book has been designed, therefore, as a programmed instructional method that will steep the beginner in disciplined play and, at the same time, pinpoint the weaknesses in an average player's game. The decisions you are asked to make throughout this text are identical to those you will make in actual play.

Poker variants covered in this book—five-card draw, five-card stud, seven-card stud, and hold 'em—are those you are most likely to encounter in serious sessions. Lowball and high-low species of each game are also examined because they are frequently added, for the sake of variety, to an evening's play.

Programmed Poker will help you establish a baseline for the mechanics of your play, an important vantage from which to evaluate and develop the psychological aspects of your style in the game.

poker

rank of hands

Although you may be dealt five, six, seven, or more cards, a poker hand always consists of five cards. Any cards not used in declaring a hand have no value whatsoever in determining a winner. Poker hands are ranked here from lowest to highest:

No pair (bust) The highest card in the no-pair hand determines its value; for example, **A 7 6 4 2** beats **K Q J 9 4.** As with any type of poker hand, completely identical hands split the pot. Poker recognizes no hierarchy of suits. (For example, **K Q J 9 4** is pronounced "king-high" or "king-high bust.")

Pair Should there be identical pairs, hands are compared for highest card, or "kicker"; for example, jacks and a queen beats jacks and a ten.

Two pair The highest pair gives the value of the hand; for example, kings and threes beats queens and tens. The kicker resolves ties. (**Q Q 10 10 4,** for example, is pronounced "queens over tens" or simply "queens-up.")

Three of a kind Ties may occur in wild-card games and, otherwise, only among very advanced players. (**9 9 9 3 K,** for example, is often pronounced "trip nines," or just "trips.")

Straight A straight is a numerical sequence of five cards in unbroken order, for example, **J 10 9 8 7.** The highest straight wins. As a rule the ace may be used both for a low straight, **A 2 3 4 5**—the "little wheel"—and for the highest straight, **10 J Q K A. (10 J Q K A,** for example, is pronounced "ace-high straight.")

Flush Any five cards all of the same suit are a flush. Flushes are ranked by the highest card; for example, an ace flush beats a king flush, a queen-nine flush beats a queen-seven flush, and so on.

Full house Also known as the "boat," this hand is composed of three of a kind plus a pair. When there are two full houses, the highest three of a kind is the winner, without regard to the pairs also present; for example, **J J J 7 7** beats **10 10 10 8 8.** (**J J J 7 7,** for example, is pronounced "jacks full of sevens" or "jacks-full.")

Four of a kind Self-explanatory and awfully impressive.

Straight flush A straight all in the same suit, this is the rarest of poker hands. The "royal flush" is an ace-high straight flush.

A "pat hand" is one that doesn't need any improvement; a full house, for example, could not reasonably be improved by drawing. Straights, flushes, full houses, four of a kind, and straight flushes are pat hands.

Quiz

Name the following assortments of cards by their proper
poker titles:

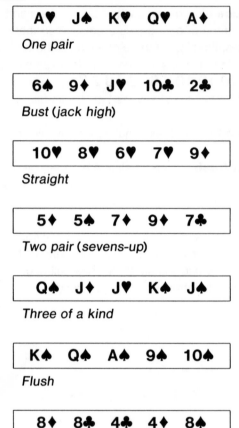

A♥ J♠ K♥ Q♥ A♦

One pair

6♠ 9♦ J♥ 10♣ 2♣

Bust (jack high)

10♥ 8♥ 6♥ 7♥ 9♦

Straight

5♦ 5♠ 7♦ 9♦ 7♣

Two pair (sevens-up)

Q♠ J♦ J♥ K♠ J♠

Three of a kind

K♠ Q♠ A♠ 9♠ 10♠

Flush

8♦ 8♣ 4♣ 4♦ 8♠

Full house (eights full)

frequencies of the hands

Poker hands are as scarce as their rank would indicate: a straight flush is the scarcest, a bust the most common. No single table can be used to give the exact frequencies (relative scarcity) of the poker-hand types in all the variants of the game. Appropriate tables accompany each game section. Raw frequency tables are not very useful, however, in actual play. It is not suggested that you try to memorize any of them. Pay somewhat closer attention to figures and tables that express "expectation of improvement" and probability of winning—these have been incorporated into the play strategy for each game.

Table 1 gives the probability of making any poker hand in exactly five cards.

TABLE 1

straight flush	64,973 to 1
four of a kind	4,164 to 1
full house	693 to 1
flush	508 to 1
straight	254 to 1
three of a kind	46 to 1
two pair	20 to 1
one pair	1.4 to 1
no pair	1 to 1

In this book, odds will be given in percentages rounded off to the nearest whole figure (except in the case of re-mote chances—the odds may be expressed in tenths of a percent or, for occurrences less than 1 in 1,000, as > 0.1%). Table 2 gives in percentages the odds shown in Table 1.

TABLE 2

straight flush	>0.1%
four of a kind	>0.1%
full house	0.1%
flush	0.2%
straight	0.4%
three of a kind	2%
two pair	5%
one pair	42%
no pair	50%

Good hands must occur more frequently when there are more hands being dealt; a hand that is less often a winner in eight-player games is more often a winner in a four-player game. Adjust your game accordingly. You will be playing eight-handed throughout this book, but you may loosen up slightly in smaller games. You may consider, in six-handed games, for example, staying on a pair of queens where previously only a pair of kings or better would do.

stakes

As a rule, no money may be wagered that was not on the table before a hand commenced.

Nearly all poker is "limit" poker. That is, no bet may exceed a predetermined limit. The number of raises also is controlled in limit poker. There are other, stiffer kinds of stakes:

Pot limit Any wager can match the amount in the pot up to that point.

No-limit or table stakes A bet can be as large as the amount the bettor has on the table. ("Table stakes" is often used only to signify that money wagered, even in a limit game, must be on the table before the deal.)

Freeze-out This does not, strictly speaking, refer to stakes, but rather to an agreement among players to sustain the game until all but one are broke. Since a game of this sort could conceivably run clear into the next tax year, the minimum bets are often raised at intervals throughout the game to facilitate heavy losing.

Buy-in Some games set a minimum beginning stake, both for convenience in disbursing the chips and in the belief that it will discourage tight players. Unless you are in a freeze-out, you may buy out at any time.

Stakes other than limit poker very much favor an experienced, psychologically adroit player; avoid these games if the description does not fit you.

Before sitting down at the table, you should provide yourself with enough money to cover the expenses you will generally incur pursuing second-best hands. Your buy-in should be not less than forty to fifty times the minimum bet. If you lose this original stake, either you are having a bad night or you may not belong in that particular game.

Do not conceive at the outset that only good players participate in high-stakes games. There is undoubtedly a law of nature that ensures, by whatever undiscovered mechanism, that nearly every poker game, regardless of stakes, state of the union, or phase of the moon, will be constituted in about the same ratio of inept to adept players.

seating

You may believe in "hot" seats and "cold" seats if you wish—since seats are neither it can't hurt you—but there is one verifiably prudent ploy in seating yourself at the table. If you have the opportunity, sit one or two seats to the left of the strongest player present. You will be informed, thus, of his intentions before you must decide on your own.

the deal

The deal passes hand by hand to the left. In "dealer's choice" the dealer calls the game to be played (but within the bounds of any agreed-upon house rules). When it is your turn to deal, shuffle two or three times, offer the deck to the player on your right for a cut, and deal *without* exposing the deck's bottom card.

When the deck is exhausted, the discards and folded hands—the deadwood—may be shuffled to provide any cards still owed active players.

betting

A small, fixed amount, called the ante, is placed in the pot before the deal by each player wishing to play. Sometimes, by agreement, the dealer antes for everyone just to speed up the play.

In stud games (games in which some cards are dealt face up) the highest card, or cards, showing have the privilege of beginning the betting. Play passes to the left from this point.

Non-stud games open with the player to the dealer's left. If the opener folds, play moves to the left. The opener retains the privilege through later rounds.

Make sure you understand the options you have when it is your turn to act; they are:

Fold You throw in your cards and leave the hand. You may fold any time it is your turn, though it makes little sense to fold if nothing has been bet prior to your turn.
Check In checking, you simply decline to bet; it is a cautious option. Naturally, you may not check if someone else has already bet.
Call If a bet has been made, you must at least put an equal amount into the pot to stay in the game. You call, or ''see,'' the bet.
Bet If you don't wish to check, you will open with a bet. The amount will be fixed by any agreed-upon limits in a particular game and by the impression you are trying to convey to your competitors.
Raise A raise is a call plus an additional wager, *usually* indicating a very strong hand. You may raise any bet when it is your turn to act, unless it would exceed any preset limit on the number of raises allowed in a round of betting.

Unless specifically prohibited, the practice of first checking and then raising in the same round, if anyone should rise to the bait, is perfectly legal. Have no qualms about ''sandbagging'' any opportunistic bettor who falls for the gambit. If you do this too often or without the finesse to precipitate an unwise bet from an outclassed opponent, you will lose money by not having bet out in the first place.

Generally any single bet is restricted to within a preset range, say between $1 and $3, on any turn. The limit is often raised for the last round of betting. Most games allow no more than three raises per round. Never be shy about asking for an explanation or clarification of the betting rules, the house rules, before getting into a game.

You cannot, incidentally, be forced out of a hand in play merely because you are out of chips. Meet as much of the bet or raise as your funds allow, and announce, probably with a catch in your throat, ''all in.'' You will be competing for as much of the pot (including your last bet) as you have participated in up to this time. Subsequent bets will be placed in a special side pot in which you have no stake and no claim. Thus, the game may have two winners: you may win the original pot, and a hand inferior to yours may win the side pot. Or you may have to borrow cab fare home.

In friendly games, players may be allowed to bet ''light,'' that is to say, bet on credit and produce any cash owed after the hand is over. To keep track of your ''lights,'' draw what you owe from the pot and pull it toward you. If you lose, this pile amounts to what you owe the winner (of course, you must pay off out of your pocket—the lights already belong to the winner). If you win, the lights are yours along with the rest of the pot.

When you bet, place the full wager all in one motion in the pot and announce the amount. You may not put a few chips in and then, as an afterthought, increase the bet (a ''string bet''). Normally, your spoken intention is a binding bet.

Quiz

If it is your turn and:

You want out of the game, you _____ .

Fold

No one has wagered yet, but you don't wish to do so, you _____ .

Check

No one has wagered yet, but you wish to do so, you

_____ .

Bet

A bet has been made, but you wish to bet a higher amount, you _____ .

Raise

A bet has been made, but you wish to bet no higher amount, you _____

Call

things that shouldn't have to be said but here they are anyway

1. "Don't play for more than you can afford to lose." Try violating this precept once or twice if you are in doubt.

2. Whatever it is we mean by "odds," it certainly does not mean that the cards turn up as if on a schedule. Things that you consider "unlikely" will, and *must,* happen over and over again. But in the ever-unfolding "long run," a presumably immortal poker player would find that everything tallies just as in our statistical ideal of the game.

3. Learning poker from a book will not make you a finished player. You must play as often as you are able. And constantly, remorselessly examine your game for its strengths and its eccentricities.

4. Study the game whenever it is played, whether you are involved in the hand or not. This much of your education, at least, is free.

5. There is no guaranteed win in poker. Period.

the two cardinal rules

Keep track of the cards Occasions will arise in stud poker when you can control and win a pot because you have remembered which key cards were in hands folded earlier. In a seven-card stud hand for instance, perhaps you hold a full house—queens full of sevens—but the indications are that you are betting against another full house made up in some ratio of kings and jacks. If you are able to remember that two visible kings were folded in the first round, you will keep raising and win a maximal amount.

It is not necessary to emblazon the cards on your memory; just pay attention to the game, and only to the game, while you are in play. Watch every up-card dealt; if the game proceeds at a smooth pace, you will probably remember what you have seen for long enough to be useful.

Hopefully, you needn't be prompted to watch for cards that affect the potential of your own hand—there is no excuse for trying to draw cards that have already been dealt to someone else. When reaching for a straight or flush, you must routinely count the unavailable members of a sequence or suit in which you have an interest.

Vary your style but not your poker Lay back deceptively with an occasional strong hand, raise with an indecipherable intent, don't be afraid to be caught in a well-timed bluff . . . but you must have a *consistent* way of evaluating your cards, deciding when to stay, how long to stay, when to raise, and when to fold—this book makes strong recommendations on precisely these points. A pair of fours, for example, does not change in value from hand to hand just because you are willing to invest more hope in them, or because your elation at winning the last hand has spilled over into the next.

If you prefer to bankroll yourself on intuition, flashes of inspiration, or sheer doggedness, you probably are, or should think of becoming, an artist—a more respectable calling for the habitually impecunious. Maintaining a poker discipline is easily the most important factor in successful play. (As has been often observed, you must make the other players try to beat your cards; don't try to beat theirs.)

five-card draw

five-card draw

Five cards are dealt face down to the players. A round of betting is initiated by the player to the dealer's left. When the initial betting is complete, remaining players—in order from the first player on the dealer's left to the last—may throw away up to three cards (up to four cards in many versions of the game) and receive new ones from the stock (the deck). A second, and final, round of betting follows. Survivors show their hands when all betting and raising has ceased. As always, best hand wins.

In one common variant of this game, a minimum opening hand is required to begin the betting. A player may be required to hold a pair, for example, of "jacks or better" to open. But only the initial bettor need hold the requisite pair. Any hand may enter the game after the ice is broken. If no one is able to open, the hand is redealt—often with an additional ante—until the opening condition is met. Openers may not be bluffed; any player is entitled to verify the openers at the conclusion of a hand. (If discarded, openers are set aside, face down, until called for.)

odds

The chances of being dealt a particular poker hand in the first five cards are given in Table 2, page 18. For the purposes of five-card draw, it is more pertinent to consider the likely state of affairs at the table *after* the draw. Predicated on more or less sensible play, Table 3 gives approximate frequencies of the hands you are apt to see at the showdown. Remember, these are much richer percentages than those going into the hand because, on the whole, only those players with something worth improving have stayed for the draw. (Few players, for example, would risk money on the 4% chance of drawing two cards to a three-card possible flush.)

TABLE 3

straight flush	>0.1%	(>0.1%)
four of a kind	0.4%	(>0.1%)
full house	2%	(0.1%)
flush	2%	(0.2%)
straight	2.5%	(0.4%)
three of a kind	12%	(2%)
two pair	23%	(5%)
one pair	47%	(42%)
no pair	11%	(50%)

(Figures in parentheses are taken from Table 2, page 18, to provide a quick comparison.)

Now that you have seen to what extent hands improve on the draw, you are probably wondering how often each kind of hand is good enough to win. That is equivalent to asking how much confidence you should have in a particular hand once you have drawn successfully. Table 4 is an acceptable approximation (calculated for the average case of a three-way showdown) of the winning percentage of each hand.

TABLE 4

straight flush	99.99+%
four of a kind	99.9+%
full house	99+%
flush	95%
straight	91%
three of a kind	87%
two pair	66%
one pair	34%
no pair	2%

Of course, it is not yet the whole story: Table 4 does not take into account the number of times, for example, that two pair wins against another two pair. You could not refer to this table with full confidence unless you held on every occasion the best possible specimen of a particular kind of hand. In practice (and theory) you won't lose a noticeable amount in head-on confrontations between straights or higher. Even in holding a low three of a kind, you need be only a little cautious about the possibility of another set of trips in the showdown. But two pair can lose to a better two pair an unprofitable number of times unless you have refined your chances by drawing only to a pair of kings or better. Aces-up is, just as in the table, a 66% winner, and kings-up are only slightly less desirable. You won't always have the opportunity to draw for kings-up or better; you may receive a middling two pair on the deal. Precisely because you will often have to play this middling two pair (after all, it's the only two pair you have), you will want the best possible chance on those occasions when you do have some choice in drawing to a single pair.

What about one pair: is a 35% chance of winning good enough to justify staying in a hand? Again, if the pair is good enough, yes. An average pot contains three times over and above what you have thrown into it. (Adjust this figure down one notch when playing five-handed or less.) Thus, the odds become prohibitive to winning at about 25%—and you would prefer as much cushion as possible above that figure. 35% is an acceptable figure if that is truly your risk, that is, if your pair is aces or kings. The percentage shrinks rapidly as the size of your pair falls.

Believe in these numbers, and play your hand accordingly, but when your alertness and good judgment have convinced you that you are beat, fold.

For your inspection and contemplation, the odds to draw at certain, useful combinations are listed in Table 5. You needn't pore over these figures: they simply identify the long shots that you will avoid in any case by studying the suggested strategy for staying and drawing presented in the next section.

TABLE 5

Drawing three cards:		
to one pair to make	two pair	16%
	trips	11%
	full house	1%
	four of a kind	0.3%
Drawing two cards:		
to one pair to make	two pair	17%
	trips	8%
	full house	0.8%
	four of a kind	0.1%
to trips to make	full house	6%
	four of a kind	4%
to three in suit to make	flush	4%
Drawing one card:		
to two pair to make	full house	9%
to trips to make	full house	6%
	four of a kind	2%
to four in suit to make	flush	19%
to four in sequence to make (open at both ends)	straight	17%
to four in broken sequence to make ("inside" straight or one-ended straight)	straight	8%

Odds quiz
Some kinds of hands are almost automatic winners;
others require work, luck, and discernment to win.
Looking at the tables, where would you draw the line
between the superior hands and the chancier hold-
ings?

The most dramatic gap occurs between two pair and three
of a kind or better.

How much better is a draw to an open, or "outside,"
straight than a draw to an inside straight or single-
ended straight?
The figures are 17% and 8%: an open draw is a little bet-
ter than twice as good as an inside draw.

What is the break-even hand in five-card draw, that
is, the lowest hand that still has any mathematical
expectation of winning more money than it loses?
A pair of kings.

Are your percentages severely compromised if you
draw only one card to trips from time to time instead
of drawing two?
No, not really; you halve your chances at a real long
shot—four of a kind—but you can afford to do this some-
times, particularly if it serves to deceive the table concern-
ing the real strength of your hand before the draw.

What hand may you expect to be a winner least
often?
No pair (2% winner).

strategy

When to stay in five-card draw:
> pair of kings or better
> jacks-up or better
> four cards to an open straight (but see appendix 1.)
> four cards to a flush (but see appendix 1.)
> three of a kind or any pat hand (this goes without saying)

Try not to arrange your cards after the deal—your meticulous regrouping of the hand could tip off your pairs or trips.

Playing two pair before the draw is a difficult business: if you could know beforehand whether there were trips anywhere around the table, you would fold without regret. But a good two pair wins the pot more often than not. What to do? No argument or strategy seems completely satisfactory. Staying on jacks-up will protect you from serious error. Trying to catch a pot with less, or to scare other contenders out with a raise, requires an experienced and sensitive estimate of the circumstances (and still fails at times when it shouldn't).

Strategy quiz

Indicate whether you will stay or fold in the following examples:

| 6♦ | 8♥ | 6♣ | 6♠ | J♠ |

Stay.

| K♥ | 8♦ | J♣ | J♦ | 9♣ |

Fold.

| 7♦ | 3♠ | 10♥ | 8♣ | J♦ |

Fold. This is an inside straight (only one card, a 9, will help); it can be made 8% of the time. An open, or outside, straight can be drawn in 17% of attempts. Please note that A 2 3 4 x and x J Q K A are also inside straights, or more properly single-ended straights, because there is only one way of connecting to the ace.

| 2♥ | A♠ | 4♥ | 3♥ | K♥ |

Stay. Of course this is a single-ended straight, but it is more notably a four-card flush. (You should throw away the ace.)

| 3♦ | K♦ | 10♣ | A♣ | 10♦ |

Fold. Drawing to a pair of tens, even with an ace kicker, won't make you any money.

the draw

Draw three cards to a pair. Your odds are not enhanced, overall, by keeping a high kicker, but you may keep the ace kicker from time to time if only to represent to other players that you hold three of a kind.

Draw one card to two pair.

Draw two cards to three of a kind. You should sometimes draw one card to this hand, particularly when your trips are of a high denomination, for the sake of making your play less predictable.

Draw one card to the four-card straight and flush; there really is no choice.

Always draw one card to a four-of-a-kind hand: you don't want to scare players away by seeming to hold a pat hand.

Quiz

Choose the best discards in the following hands:

Q♣ 6♣ 7♣ Q♦ A♦

Keep the queens, and keep the ace kicker on occasion.

8♣ 9♦ 9♣ 4♥ 4♦

Keep the two pair; they're a weak two pair, but there are no other options.

K♥ 9♥ K♣ 6♥ 4♥

It's a good set of openers—but what to throw away? Should you destroy your pair to draw for the flush? Keep the kings. The flush would be more certainly a winner, but the hand you hold is nearly 35% a winner and has better than a 28% combined chance of improvement as against only 19% of successful draws to the flush. In a hand of "jacks or better," you may opt for a flush draw if the opener drew only two cards.

5♣ 6♣ 4♣ 8♣ 7♦

A pat hand at last. If you wanted to throw away the diamond and draw to the flush, return to the bookstore and try earnestly to get your money back.

betting

Before the draw: don't raise before the draw except with aces-up or low trips—they are good hands, and you wish to discourage low pairs from staying and outdrawing you. Call a raise if you have a pat hand, trips, or aces-up.

After the draw: check and call with one or two pair or middling trips; bet or raise with anything higher.

Betting strategy is never an invariable formula. Pay attention to the game and the players. You will often find yourself betting higher or lower (or folding) on the basis of assumptions you have made during the evolution of an actual hand. This is fine and profitable so long as you finance only your most confident assumptions.

An example: you hold queens-up; two players ahead of you have drawn only two cards. The first may well have kept a kicker, but the second draws with the knowledge he may be up against trips—he certainly can't hope to win by drawing to a kicker; therefore he, at least, has trips already. You should fold. (Don't enter a hand when you know you are outclassed; most of the time, the draw will not repair your disadvantage.)

play of the game

In the complete hands that follow, you will be asked to indicate your actions with **fold, check, call, bet,** or **raise** on a separate sheet of paper. The correct answer is indicated in the first column. The best choice—where there is any doubt—and the reasons for it will be found underneath the correct answer. Only those plays that come in turn before yours will be given in each frame; thus, you will have as much information as you would in actual play. If a raise should occur after your turn, this will appear in a subsequent section of the frame. As always, you will wish to use your answer sheet to conceal the answers until you have arrived at your own.

Among other things in five-card draw, you will probably find that the course of a hand offers you very few clues to your opponents' holdings. As compared with stud games, you play in the dark. You will attach greater importance, therefore, to the sheer percentage value of your hand; in stud games this general percentage value can be improved upon—it may grow or wane, depending on what you find in the exposed cards of the other players.

FIRST GAME

You	Vinnie	Emma	Marv	Lefty	Roxy	Silvio	Claire
2♣ A♦ **A♣ K♡** **4♣**							
			bet	call	fold	fold	call
call							
The draw:							
6♡ 6♦ **J♠**	one		one	two			three
Second round:							
			bet	fold			raise
call							

Call the raise. You could be up against trips, but never fold aces-up to someone who drew three. As a matter of fact, everyone else folds (Lefty didn't improve his pair-with-kicker) except Marv. Claire holds kings-up, Marv has a weak two pair, and you are the winner.

Aces-up is such a high percentage winner that you should fold it only when a quick review of the draw and the betting leads you to the certain conclusion that it's insufficient for the hand in progress.

SECOND GAME

You	Vinnie	Emma	Marv	Lefty	Roxy	Silvio	Claire
8♡ 9♦ **6♦ 9♠** **6♣**							
					bet	call	fold
call							
	raise	call			call	call	
fold							

The two pair you are working with aren't very distinguished—too many players were willing to see the raise, and Vinnie didn't seem to mind at all jumping into the pot *after* it had become expensive. Nothing less than a full house can help you, and that's a 9% chance; no eight-handed game could possibly pay you back for the risk.

THIRD GAME

You	Vinnie	Emma	Marv	Lefty	Roxy	Silvio	Claire
6♠ 7♠ **A♦ A♣** **4♡**		bet	call	call	fold	fold	call
call							
The draw:							
J♡ K♠ **2♣**		three	one	two			one
Second round:							
		check	bet	raise			reraise
fold							

No way. Lefty, who has trips, thinks Marv has two pair, and both must now ask themselves searching questions about Claire's draw. But not you; you are safely out of it.

FOURTH GAME

You	Vinnie	Emma	Marv	Lefty	Roxy	Silvio	Claire
K♤ 7♢ **K♢ 9♡** **8♡**							
		bet	fold	call	fold	fold	fold
call							

The draw:

10♢ 9♧ **2♡**		three		three			

Only two other players, and both drawing three. You had the best hand going in.

Second round:

		check		bet			
call							

Don't raise; Lefty may have got lucky. More probably he's decided his jacks are just good enough for this hand. They aren't.

FIFTH GAME

You	Vinnie	Emma	Marv	Lefty	Roxy	Silvio	Claire
8♧ A♢ **9♧ 4♧** **6♤** (the age)							
check							

No need to fold right off the bat; wait until someone opens.

	check	check	check	bet	fold	call	fold

Now fold.

SIXTH GAME

You	Vinnie	Emma	Marv	Lefty	Roxy	Silvio	Claire
J♠ 8♡ 2♢ J♡ 4♢							
			check	check	check	check	
bet							

This is not strictly according to the book, but it is good poker. With such a lack of enthusiasm around the table, you are relatively safe in overrepresenting your hand. Watch out for Vinnie and Emma, who haven't spoken yet.

	raise	fold	fold	fold	fold	fold	call
call							

Under the circumstances, Vinnie's raise is likely to spring from the same motive as your own opening bet—a raise at the end of a long line of checked hands almost never indicates strength. (If the raiser really held anything, he would worry about driving players out of his pot, and the calls on your bet are the best return he could hope for.)

The draw:

K♠ 6♠	three						three

You can draw three cards, of course, but you might as well noise the idea about that you have trips. (Don't do this too often.)

Second round:

							check
bet							

Emma folded; Claire called with jacks and a queen kicker. Your king was an inspired draw. Though not very profitable, this has been a very useful hand: the opposition is puzzled by the showdown. Did you keep a king kicker, or bluff trips?

SEVENTH GAME

You	Vinnie	Emma	Marv	Lefty	Roxy	Silvio	Claire
J◇ 8◇ 10♤ 9♤ 3♡ (the age)							
check	check	bet	call	raise	call	call	fold
call							
The pot is large enough to offset your 17% chance at a straight.							
The draw:							
7♤		one	three	none	one	two	
Second round:							
check							
Check to a raiser who draws no cards unless you have a full house.							
		check	check	bet	fold	call	
call							
As it happens, Lefty holds a low club flush. The straight will win often, just not this time.							

EIGHTH GAME

You	Vinnie	Emma	Marv	Lefty	Roxy	Silvio	Claire
10♡ 3♤ **5♡ 2♡** **K♡**							
			bet	fold	call	call	call
call							
This hand promises stakes high enough to justify the flush draw. (See appendix 1.)							
The draw:							
K♢	two		one		three	one	three
Second round:							
			check		check	bet	raise
fold							
The kings come too late. At least a good two pair is present in the betting. (You might consider staying in quieter circumstances.)							

lowball

Lowball is upside-down poker: the lowest hand wins. Hands are rated by the highest low card; for example, **8 7 3 2 A** is an "eight-low," but is also called an "eight-high" or an "eight-six." The hand **8 5 3 2 A** is also an eight-low but a lower one than the first example and, hence, a winner. (The higher of the two hands would be termed a "rough" eight; the lower is a "smooth" eight.) Straights and flushes do not count in a lowball hand; **2 3 4 5 6** is both a straight and an impressive low hand.

odds

The odds in lowball are shown in Tables 6 and 7.

TABLE 6

any pair or higher (straights and flushes excluded)	
	49%
king-high	20%
queen-high	13%
jack-high	8%
ten-high	5%
nine-high	3%
eight-high	1%
seven-high	0.6%
six-high	0.2%
five-high	>0.1%

TABLE 7

Odds for an improved, unpaired low, drawing one card to a hand that was dealt as:	
any pair	77%
king-high	68%
queen-high	59%
jack-high	51%
ten-high	43%
nine-high	34%
eight-high	26%
seven-high	17%
six-high	9%
five-high	cannot be improved

Table 7 should suggest to you that there is little profit in drawing to a ten-high or lower. The figures illustrate that in lowball there are no clear-cut, obvious stages in the draw to cut off your play; the numbers progress in smooth increments from highest to lowest. If you can't always be dealt a pat hand, say ten-high or lower, then try to stay on as low a second-highest card as possible. That is, **K 8 6 4 5** is infinitely better than **K Q 3 2 4.**

Just for laughs, the odds to draw *two* cards at a low hand are given in Table 8.

TABLE 8

Drawing two cards to end up with a:	
nine-low	15%
eight-low	8%
seven-low	3%
six-low	1%

There are no excuses for drawing two cards to a potential lowball hand.

strategy

Lowball has become something of a poker specialty. This game is more speculative, and hence more rewarding to the player with an experienced, psychological edge, than most variants. The advice offered here will enable you to keep ahead of the occasional lowball hand that arises out of dealer's choice situations.

As we have surmised from the foregoing tables, it can't pay to draw more than one card to a low hand. In this game, the draw is as likely to bring sudden reverses as to bring any help. You are better off with a pat hand, and pretty much in control with a seven-low or better. A strictly lowball hand has not the same feel as high poker; every player who stays for the draw is looking for the same kind of hand. You will not be the beneficiary, by default, of busted straights and flushes, or a failed two pair. So:

1. Never draw more than one card, and fold if it doesn't revolutionize your hand.
2. Strongly consider staying on a smooth ten or better, but don't do anything pyrotechnical in the betting unless you hold a seven-low or better.

betting

Betting is not complicated. You must bet out when your hand looks good and back off when uncertain. It's the only way you will win enough on your good hands to pay for all the quick turnarounds in this game.

Lowball quiz

Since you won't be drawing more than one card to a strictly lowball hand, indicate whether you stay or fold for the following hands:

10♥ 2♦ 9♥ J♦ 3♦

Fold. It's a rough ten in the most optimistic draw.

6♣ 3♣ K♦ 5♦ 7♣

Stay.

2♥ A♥ 4♥ J♦ Q♦

Fold. A jack is usually just too high.

10♣ 2♠ 7♦ 4♥ 5♣

Stay. The real problem here is whether to draw or not. In the absence of any additional information, consider standing pat on this relatively smooth ten.

2♠ 3♦ 4♦ 6♣ 5♣

Stay. A sure winner; remember, straights are not disqualified.

five-card draw high-low

In a high-low game, the pot is split fifty-fifty between the highest and lowest hand. Although you may think that winning half a pot is scarcely worth the risk, the pots are generally larger than in high poker because players develop two divergent sets of aspirations—and some players stay on the ineffectual premise that a middling hand will somehow acquire a direction and stature.

strategy

Do not stay unless you have a clear intention to win either high or low. You may occasionally win both ends of the pot if you have stayed on a bona-fide low hand that develops into a low straight or flush.

As with lowball, straights and flushes may generally be disregarded for the purposes of declaring a low hand. Inquire before the deal about the rank of straights and flushes if you are not sure how a particular group of players is using the cards.

Playing with a "declaration" (refer to the section "seven-card stud high-low") is unusual in five-card draw.

In the following high-low split hands, fill in the blanks with your intention to stay or fold, and if you stay, which end of the pot will you aspire to? Lastly, what card or cards will you throw away?

High-low quiz

4♣	J♣	3♦	2♣	J♥

Stay or fold? High or low? Discards?
Fold. These are the beginnings of a classic second-best hand; it's neither high nor low in a convincing way.

6♦	5♥	A♣	K♣	2♣

Stay or fold? High or low? Discards?
Stay. Low. King.

4♠	3♥	5♥	2♠	7♣

Stay or fold? High or low? Discards?
Stay. Low. None.

K♠	3♦	4♣	A♥	K♥

Stay or fold? High or low? Discards?
Stay. High. **3♦ 4♣ A♥**

4♦	A♥	3♥	2♥	A♣

Stay or fold? High or low? Discards?
Stay. High or low. An ace or **3♥ 4♦ 2♥**. *Both alternatives are quite good. Perhaps the play preceding yours will have given you some ideas as to which end to aim at. Although the low version of your hand has a remote possibility (single-ended straight) of capturing the whole pot and is a good low draw, still the pair of aces is a pretty safe way to go about winning the high end. It's a tough decision; in whatever direction you go you are neither convicted nor exonerated.*

6♦	7♦	7♥	5♣	A♣

Stay or fold? High or low? Discards?
Stay. Low. A seven.

Q♣   10♠   8♠   9♥   6♣

Stay or fold? High or low? Discards?

*Fold. This is an inside straight for the high end and only a
ten-nine-low plus the hazard of a draw for the low end.* Two
chances at mediocre hands aren't somehow better than one shot
at filling a mediocre hand. *Reasonable players do not become
excited at doubling up their chances to make a losing hand.*

five-card stud

five-card stud

Two cards—one up, one down—are dealt in the first round; betting ensues. A third, fourth, and fifth exposed card are dealt with a round of betting after each.

odds

Because there is no opportunity to exchange unwanted cards and no extra cards, this is the most straightforward of all poker games. A hand that is just plain insufficient in other forms of poker may be your bread and butter here.

If everyone just sat at the table and waited for the first five cards to be dealt, the occurrences of hands in five-card stud would conform exactly to Table 2, page 18. That's not how the game is played. Because players fold or stay on the promise of their initial holdings and subsequent acquisitions, you are likely to see at the showdown the distribution of hands given in Table 9.

TABLE 9

no pair	36%
one pair	55%
two pair	6%
three of a kind	3%
full house	0.3%
four of a kind	>0.1%

You are probably wondering how to go about making a straight or flush in five-card stud. The truth is you shouldn't try. Of those hands that begin as two-card segments of possible straights and flushes, only 3% and 1% respectively will draw out. There is no way to compensate you for those odds. It can happen, but rarely, that you complete a straight or flush while drawing to an unpaired assortment of high cards. If you find yourself holding four cards to an open straight or a flush, by all means stay for the fifth.

Table 10 shows the percentage of cases in which you may expect to win in a three-way showdown (but remember, it's out of an eight-handed game), when you hold the *best possible* kind of:

TABLE 10

no pair	13%
one pair	82%
two pair	94%
three of a kind	99%
full house	99.9+%
four of a kind	99.99+%

If you are thinking it doesn't pay to call the last bet holding an unpaired assortment, you are right. But players do it when they can't see any exposed pairs and hold an ace—no money in this kind of play. There is no objection, of course, to staying on no pair when the last round is a free ride (that is, when the surviving hands check all around), a not uncommon occurrence in five-card stud.

You can justify 83% confidence in a pair only when they are aces, and a little less when they are kings. *The higher the cards you play for, the better your chances of winning.* Because two pair and three of a kind are dramatically less frequent hands in five-card stud, you will be rewarded by placing some confidence in nearly any example of the species. Be cautious only when there is a developing, visible threat to your hopes.

A high pair or middling two pair is far and away the majority winner in this game.

The odds for improving good openers are given in Table 11.

TABLE 11

Holding a wired pair:	
no improvement	72%
two pair	16%
three of a kind	11%
full house	1%
four of a kind	0.2%

Holding **A x** or **K x**:	
no pair	54%
any pair	40%
(pair of **A**s or **K**s	13%)
(pair of any **x**	27%)
two pair	4%
three of a kind	2%
full house	0.2%
four of a kind	>0.1%

Naturally, you would rather hold a wired pair every time you entered the game, but wired pairs are only dealt 6% of the time. It is worth your while to get into the game with an ace or king, and with both an ace and king on the deal, to stay for the hand.

Odds quiz

How good do you think your chances are to win with a single pair of aces and a queen kicker (assume you are not beat in sight)?
About 83%.

How are your chances with a single pair of eights?
The tables don't say, but it's in the neighborhood of 40% or less.

The expectations you have been given are for winning a three-way showdown. In which direction should the percentages be adjusted if more players stay for the showdown?
You should lower your expectation of winning with each additional player over three staying in the showdown. It's not possible to construct a meaningful table for large showdowns because the simple fact of their occurrence usually (but how "usually"?) indicates the presence of one, and often two (but how "often"?), superior hands at the table.

Looking at the table for hand distribution (Table 9), where would you say the line should be drawn between "risky" and "rewarding" hands?
Two pair and higher are rewarding, and you may safely include pairs of aces and kings in that category.

If the expectation of winning is, at best, 13% holding no pair, why would anyone stay for the showdown with this hand?
There are a number of acceptable situations: 1) not beaten in sight, and holding an ace, a free ride in the last round; 2) holding four cards higher than any open pair, and a free ride in the last round; 3) holding an ace and believing, on the evidence of the betting, that no one has paired.

strategy

When to stay after the deal:

A K   27% chance of pairing one of them; stay for the hand.

A x

K x—Stay when no ace is showing.

Any wired pair.

After the third card:

A x x or **K x x**—Fold if beaten by any open pair.

Keep a wired pair until beaten in sight.

After the fourth card:

A x x x—Stay if all of your unpaired cards are higher than any open pair and only if the pot offers you at least a 3 to 1 return on your investment.

After the fifth card:

Get out if unpaired and forced to call a bet.

Strategy quiz

Indicate whether you would stay or fold with the following openers:

A♣ K♥	7♦ 7♥	Q♠ J♣	K♦ 9♦	J♣ J♦
Stay.	Stay.	Fold.	Stay if no ace is showing.	Stay.

9♠ 8♠	A♥ 6♦	3♦ K♥	Q♦ J♦	10♣ A♠
Fold.	Stay.	Stay if no ace is showing.	Fold.	Stay.

the hole card

You may hear players discussing the pros and cons of having your high card, the ace or king, dealt in the concealed position. Although it is undoubtedly emotionally reassuring to have an "ace in the hole," it has no clear advantage over an exposed ace. Don't change your betting behavior on this account. On balance, for every occasion the concealed card gives you a "sleeping" winner, the exposed high card gives you critical leverage in the betting—forcing other hands out of the game, or into cautious acquiescence—allowing you to improve your hand at little cost. Used with the proper timing and élan, an exposed high card can make a successful bluff. An ace in the hole, by contrast, often encourages inexperienced players to stay in a hand they should have dropped. Think of an ace in the hole just in the sense in which it has entered the language, that is, to mean the resolution of a desperate situation. The hand is a good one, but without magical powers.

Play of the game

On a separate sheet of paper, select **fold, check, call, bet,** or **raise,** as you deem appropriate.

FIRST GAME

You	Vinnie	Emma	Marv	Lefty	Roxy	Silvio	Claire
A♦ K♥	10♣	10♠	7♥	4♠	Q♣	9♥	2♦
bet							
There aren't many better opening hands in five-card stud.							
	fold	fold	fold	fold	call	call	call
A♥					7♣	8♦	5♦
bet							
					call	call	call
J♠					Q♦	4♣	5♠
					bet	fold	call
raise							
You have the hand won at this stage, and everyone has the same chance at two pair, so bet it that way.							
9♦					check		bet
call							
Don't raise the raiser with a single pair; Claire knows you raised last time, and still she raises. She shouldn't have been in this hand at all, but wins with twos and fives. It happens.							

SECOND GAME

You	Vinnie	Emma	Marv	Lefty	Roxy	Silvio	Claire
J♡ J♣	6♦	A♦	K♣	9♠	10♠	3♥	K♠
		bet	call	fold	fold	fold	call
call							

Looks pretty good. You should be mildly curious as to why both kings stayed—there are only so many kings to go around.

9♦		Q♥	4♣				9♣
		bet	fold				call
call							

You're hoping but a long way from collecting. It appears both kings suffered a lapse of judgment, and Marv, at least, has realized he stayed for one card too many.

10♥		K♥					9♥
							bet
call							

No reason to leave yet.

		raise					call
call							

A grim turn of events, but your jacks are still very much alive, alive enough to call the raise.

4♦		J♠					2♥
							check
check							

You must also check to the raiser and her looming straight or high pair, but she checks too. She has missed pairing any of her high cards and felt a final bet would be an amateurish bluff under the circumstances. Your jacks win; Claire was never really in this pot.

THIRD GAME

You	Vinnie	Emma	Marv	Lefty	Roxy	Silvio	Claire
4♦ A♦	3♣	K♠	4♥	9♠	J♣	Q♠	Q♥
bet							
	fold	call	fold	call	call	fold	fold
4♣		9♥		8♣	J♥		
					bet		
fold							

This situation is frequently encountered in five-card stud. Your odds (taking into account the cards we can see) to make two pair are 22%, trips 5%, full house 0.8%. If all three of your opponents stay for the showdown, you have perhaps a net profit of 2% or less (you must win 25% of the time in a four-way hand to break even; profit is over and above that 25% and is always less than the net odds—2.8% in this case—merely to make a hand). If you decide to play this kind of hand, that is, *playing from behind,* only when there are five or six players in the pot, then the sufficiency of two pair *to win* is correspondingly reduced because of the presence of more players drawing to trips or better. In general, *do not stay when you are beat in sight.*

FOURTH GAME

You	Vinnie	Emma	Marv	Lefty	Roxy	Silvio	Claire
K♥ Q♠	9♠	J♣	5♦	9♦	A♣	4♠	2♣
					bet	fold	fold
call							
J♥		8♠			10♦		
					bet		
call							

Only three of you left in the pot, and you are drawing to respectable cards.

A♥		10♣			K♥		
bet							

You are testing the hypothesis that yours is the best hand at this point. Emma and Roxy call.

3♦		6♦			2♠		
check							

Your **A K Q** beats Roxy's **A K 10** and Emma's **A J.** Anyone might have paired the hole card on the last round, so you really shouldn't bet out.

FIFTH GAME

You	Vinnie	Emma	Marv	Lefty	Roxy	Silvio	Claire
10♣ 10♥	A♣	2♦	3♦	8♣	Q♥	Q♠	Q♦
	bet	fold	fold	fold	fold	fold	fold
call							
4♦	A♠						
	bet						
fold							

A two-way confrontation with a pair of aces? You are drawing from a distinctly inferior position to win a slender pot that couldn't possibly pay you back for your troubles (as the hand now stands, your chances for trip tens—the closest thing to a sure winner—are less than 10%).

SIXTH GAME

You	Vinnie	Emma	Marv	Lefty	Roxy	Silvio	Claire
K◇ K♠	9♠	2♦	A♣	2♥	Q♥	J♥	10♦
			bet	fold	call	fold	call
call							

You have a percentage "lock" on this hand. You could have raised, but you may make more money if you wait one round. Vary your play (see the two cardinal rules, page 24).

J♠	6♦		7♥		9♣		K♣
			bet		call		call
raise							

If you didn't do it last time, do it now.

J♦			K♥		10♣		4♦
bet							

Everyone folds. In a way the pair of jacks have hurt you—the table now has you figured for trip jacks. To check at this point wouldn't help because Marv, Roxy, and Claire will just fold in the next round when you begin to rattle your chips (not to mention the fact that you would present them with a free opportunity to draw to any long shots among them). *As a rule, you must bet your hand to make money.*

SEVENTH GAME

You	Vinnie	Emma	Marv	Lefty	Roxy	Silvio	Claire
9♡ 9♠	6♣	2♦	A♦	J♠	6♥	5♣	Q♥
			bet	call	fold	fold	call
call							
J♣			4♦	10♥			8♦
			bet	call			call
call							

(You are far from beat yet; although Lefty now has two cards that could better your pair, you are holding one of the cards he needs.)

You	Vinnie	Emma	Marv	Lefty	Roxy	Silvio	Claire
8♣			6♠	9♣			8♥
							bet
call							
			fold	raise			call
call							

As unlikely as it may seem, Lefty appears to have paired the nines. Hang on, and hope for a respectable kicker.

You	Vinnie	Emma	Marv	Lefty	Roxy	Silvio	Claire
K♦				A♣			5♦
							check
check							

And Lefty checks too. His hole card was a queen; he was playing for a straight all along. (If Lefty does this very often in five-card stud, you should write his name down in a book somewhere so you will be sure to remember to invite him to all the games.) You win.

EIGHTH GAME

You	Vinnie	Emma	Marv	Lefty	Roxy	Silvio	Claire
9♡ 9♣	4♥	6♦	K♠	10♣	A♠	8♣	A♦
					bet	fold	call
call							
9♠			Q♣		A♥		10♦
					bet		call
call							

Don't raise yet. Trips are such a sure thing in five-card stud that you must conceal them for the present and be thankful that Marv and Claire haven't folded yet; if they weren't intimidated by Roxy's aces, they certainly would be by a raise from your nines. You do not bet your hand yet precisely because you are letting Roxy do it for you.

You	Vinnie	Emma	Marv	Lefty	Roxy	Silvio	Claire
8♥			3♣		K♦		10♥
					bet		call
raise							

Pay attention: both Roxy and Claire have pairs superior to yours; it is safe to assume they will stay for the fifth card (one of them may even win). Marv has collapsed on fourth street.

You	Vinnie	Emma	Marv	Lefty	Roxy	Silvio	Claire
8♦					A♣		9♦
					bet		fold
raise							

A full house in five-card stud is better than a cashier's check.

five-card stud low

Five-card stud low is simply low poker dealt in the five-card stud format. Hands are ranked as in lowball; lowest assortment wins.

strategy

You may play five-card stud low in a looser way than lowball. For one thing, you have more information about your opponents' hands. There is very little strategy involved in this game: fold when you can see you are beat, bet when you're not. Don't stay after the deal if your hole card plus your up card total more than ten; no pairs. However, if your open card is an ace or deuce against a generally middling to high table, you may well force them all out of the game regardless of your hole card's value.

(Five-card stud is rarely played as a high-low split game; if you should play this variant, you are reminded to aim at one end or the other and not in between.)

Openers quiz

Will you stay or fold in five-card stud low with these sample openers?

6♡ 3♦	2♤ 9♥	2♧ 6♣	A♡ Q♦
Stay.	*Fold.*	*Stay.*	*Fold.*

A♤ 9♠	2♡ 4♥	8♤ A♠	10♡ 5♦
Stay.	*Stay.*	*Stay.*	*Fold.*

J♧ A♦

Questionable. You may wish to stay occasionally on this sort of hand. The rest of the table doesn't know your hole card is high. If theirs are creeping upward on the draw and yours stay low, you have acquired leverage. Bet out as long as your cards hold.

Play of the game

Once again, commit yourself, in writing, to **fold, check, call, bet,** or **raise.**

FIRST GAME

You	Vinnie	Emma	Marv	Lefty	Roxy	Silvio	Claire
6♣ 2♥	9♣	4♠	Q♠	K♦	5♥	9♥	A♦
							bet
call							
7♦		3♣			8♦		J♠
		bet			call		fold
call							
5♣		5♦			3♥		
		bet			call		
call							
Q♦		7♣			K♥		
		bet			call		
fold							

If you can't see a pair in Emma's hand, then there is only a 17% chance that the hole card is paired. Roxy is either unaware of this distressing statistic or has spotted something in Emma's play that led her to call the last bet. Emma, in fact, had paired her three some time back; Roxy wins.

SECOND GAME

You	Vinnie	Emma	Marv	Lefty	Roxy	Silvio	Claire
Q♡ A♦	10♣	6♥	Q♣	J♣	8♣	Q♦	8♠
bet							

Cards around the table are rather high—this could work. You may fold, of course; that is the safe play.

7♦	9♦	K♠			3♣		5♦
bet							

2♥	9♠				7♣		J♦
bet							

You must bet here knowing full well that Roxy, at least, and probably Claire will stay for the last card. Your purpose is not to scare them away (which you can't do in this late round), but to avoid showing weakness by checking. No money is likely to be saved by checking anyway, as Roxy would only bet out in the vacuum created by your check.

2♦					8♦		4♠
							bet
fold							

Well, it didn't work; Claire hasn't attracted a pair. Roxy again calls an unpaired hand, this time holding an open pair herself, and loses the money she won from Emma a while back. If you almost called, out of "curiosity," take a second look at Roxy's chips as they go westward over the edge of the table.

THIRD GAME

You	Vinnie	Emma	Marv	Lefty	Roxy	Silvio	Claire
7◇ 2♦	4♠	2♣	8♣	J♣	J♠	A♠	Q♦
						bet	fold
call							
5♥	10♣	K♥	3♣			8♦	
bet							
4♦	J♦	K♠	7♥			2♥	
bet							
As with most low poker hands, it all comes down to the last card.							
6♦	2♠		7♣			3♠	
bet							
	call		call			raise	
reraise							

Silvio's cards haven't been running well tonight, and he has decided his genuine eight-low has just got to be a winner (it's a good enough hand in the abstract, but he should have respected your very real, exposed cards). You are seldom offered a chance to make money without risk; don't shrink from the opportunity.

FOURTH GAME

You	Vinnie	Emma	Marv	Lefty	Roxy	Silvio	Claire
A♣ 7♣	K♠	K♦	5♣	8♠	9♥	4♠	J♣
			bet	fold	call	call	fold
call							
8♦			9♠		6♥	J♥	
bet							
Bet 'em when you got 'em in this game.							
7♦			Q♥		5♦	10♠	
					bet	call	
fold							
Yours has become a middling hand. It is very probable that at least one of the three hands remaining in play will not turn up a pair, and about half of those pairs would slide in under yours anyway.							

seven-card stud

seven-card stud

Two cards down and one card face up are dealt each player; the opening bets are made. Three more cards are dealt face up, with a round of betting after each. The seventh, and last, card is dealt face down, and the final round of betting begins. In the showdown, only the best *five-card* poker hand is selected from among the seven cards held by each of the active players. The best of the hands wins the pot.

frequencies of the hands

Because each player is entitled to seven cards, from which he will select the best five-card hand, *good hands are much more likely to be dealt in seven-card stud than in five-card games*. Seven cards dealt straight from the deck would produce, on the average, the proportions of five-card poker hands shown in Table 12.

TABLE 12

no pair	16%
one pair	41%
two pair	23%
three of a kind	5%
straight (not a misprint, but see appendix 2.)	8%
flush	4%
full house	3%
four of a kind	0.2%
straight flush	>0.1%

The actual occurrence of hands—since unpromising cards are mostly folded before the showdown—is a different thing entirely. The figures in Table 13, compiled from a thousand complete games, show how often you may expect to see a particular type of winning hand (how often does two pair win? a flush?).

In parentheses are the odds on a showdown between two best hands of the same type, an ace flush beating a queen flush, for example. As you can see, this is a significant factor for one of the more common hands—such as two pair—and the reason that you will be advised not to stay with less than kings-up. Such considerations are relatively remote when you are holding a full house, although you will occasionally lose to a better example of the full house. But with any type of hand, the higher your specimen, the greater are your chances of winning.

TABLE 13

no pair	0.7%	(100%)
one pair	19%	(67%)
two pair	34%	(30%)
three of a kind	12%	(11%)
straight	10%	(6%)
flush	11%	(13%)
full house	12%	(5%)
four of a kind	0.8%	(0%)
straight flush	0.1%	(0%)

You must not think that one pair is a good bet merely because it ekes out a win in 19% of the deals—usually these involve showdowns in which several players were aiming at flushes or straights, or an unimproved set of aces or kings sufficed to take the pot. As you will see in

Table 14, one pair is second best about four times as often as it is a winner.

Table 14 expresses the ratio of the number of times a type of hand wins to the total number of times it appears in the showdown. You may consider this table as a measure of the degree of confidence you should have in a specific kind of hand. It is obvious that a player with a full house can proceed with near certainty of winning the pot. In fact, the problem with such a hand is less one of winning than of maximizing your winnings through shrewd betting.

TABLE 14

no pair	6%
one pair	28%
two pair	55%
three of a kind	68%
straight	76%
flush	77%
full house	94%
four of a kind	$\cong$100%
straight flush	$\cong$100%

Approximate odds for improving some promising three-, four-, and five-card hands are given in Table 15. These expectations are built into the seven-card stud strategy developed in the next few pages.

TABLE 15

Holding three cards, including a pair, and drawing to:	
two pair	37%
three of a kind	10%
full house	7%
four of a kind	0.5%
Holding three cards that make three of a kind, and drawing to:	
full house	33%
four of a kind	8%
Holding three cards, either in sequence or in suit, and drawing to:	
straight*	21%
flush	18%
Holding four cards, that make two pair, and drawing to:	
full house	20%
four of a kind	0.5%
Holding four cards all in sequence or in suit, and drawing to:	
straight*	36%
flush	40%
Holding four cards, three of which are in sequence or in suit, and drawing to:	
straight*	14%
flush	10%

Holding five cards, four of which are in sequence or in suit, and drawing to:	
straight*	29%
flush	32%

*Halve these odds for drawing to an inside or a single-ended straight.

how visible cards affect the odds

The cards you can see on the table can have an important bearing on your decision to pursue a hand or give it up. To present an extreme example, if you hold four spades, but there are nine spades visible in other hands, your chances of making a spade flush are exactly zero. In computing the odds for expectation, given in Table 15, we have used an average figure. That is, we have assumed that the cards you need are visibly present in open hands in about the same proportion they are present in a complete deck. Any suit makes up 25% of the deck; when you can see—referring to the example above—that more than a quarter of the visible cards are spades, your odds to make the flush begin to decrease. If you can see only three spades (counting your own, of course) out of, say, fifteen visible cards—that's only 20%—then your odds become *better* than what you have read in the table above. (25% is about the right figure for an open straight also; use it for your computations.)

In practice, such calculations should be performed at the third or fourth card and, usually, only for the case of an impending straight or flush. You will generally pursue other kinds of hands—a high two pair is a good example—relying more on their immediate value than on a strong promise of improvement.

Odds quiz

What is the minimum hand with a better than fifty-fifty prospect of winning?
A high two pair.

True or false: there is no reason to fear betting a full house into a better full house, because it happens so infrequently.
True.

All things being equal, which is the better draw, one to a straight or one to a flush?
One to a flush.

What do you think "all things being equal" in the above question could mean?
That both of the drawing hands can see an equal number of the cards they need turned up on the table.

True or false: trips are a good hand.
Yes, but don't overplay them.

You hold 4 5 6 7; on the board are two eights. Are your chances to make the straight average, better than average, or worse?
Not enough information; you need to know how many visible cards are on the table.

Assume, in the preceding question, that sixteen cards (including two of your own) are showing. Are your chances average, above average, or worse?
Average; 4/16 = 1/4 or 25%—remember it either way you wish.

The lower the percentage of visible cards that you need, the _____ your chances to draw your hand.
Higher.

strategy

When to stay after the deal:

x x y (low pair)—Stay for one card.

A K x—Stay for one card.

A A x or **K K x**—Stay for the hand.

x x x (any trips)—Stay for the hand.

three cards in suit or sequence—Stay for one card. (You may wait for two cards, if you're just trying to keep busy, but the odds are distinctly unfavorable.) *Fold all other hands.*

On the fourth card:

A K x—Must pair a high card, preferably, or fold.

x x y—Must make three of a kind or fold. (If you make two low pair on the fourth card and stay to draw the boat, make sure the pot justifies the risk— 20%; you need four other bettors and none of your cards visible.)

four cards in suit or sequence—Stay for the hand.

On the fifth card:

Nothing happens here unless you are still waiting for your fourth card in sequence or suit—unwise.

On the sixth card:

If you have stayed this far for good and sufficient cause, there is no decision to be made at this point. *Buying the last card is the least expensive investment you'll make.*

On the seventh card:

Stay for the showdown with two good pair or three of a kind if you are not obviously outclassed (when, for example, you are caught in a crossfire between convincing straights and flushes). Fold anything higher than three of a kind only for the most insistent of forebodings.

Strategy quiz

Will you stay or fold, given the following openers?

10♡ 10♢ 6♣

Stay, for one card at least.

9♤ J♡ Q♠

Fold. No good; inside straight.

2♧ 6♡ 2♥

Fold, unless you're superstitious about deuces. Then, by all means, stay.

A♡ A♤ A♣

You've hit the mother lode.

5♢ 2♢ K♦

Stay. One card.

Stay. One card.

Staying for more than the fourth card is more than a casual commitment in seven-card stud. Because it is so important, look at the four-card assortments below, and decide whether you will fold or continue.

6♡ 7♡ Q♥ 3♦

Fold is best; go looking for the fourth heart at your own expense.

5♦ 7♤ 6♠ 3♥

Inside straight; fold.

10♤ 6♦ 10♣ 6♣

Your choice. It really depends on how you assess the table.

8♣ 8♦ Q♥ 10♠

Fold. You probably shouldn't have entered this hand anyway.

A♣ A♦ 6♠ 2♥

Stay until you are sure you are beat.

A♡ K♡ 7♠ Q♣

Fold.

7♣ Q♣ 9♣ 3♣

Stay for the rest of the hand.

Lastly, before we leap into the complexities of playing with seven cards, find the best poker hand in these last-round assortments. Everyone has miscalled a hand at one time or another and lost money. When the house rules permit, make a habit of turning up your full, seven-card hand at the showdown so the dealer can check it for any possibilities you may have missed.

9♦ 9♠ Q♠ J♠ 9♥ 8♣ 10♠

This is three of a kind, but you'll win more if you identified it as a queen-high straight.

| A♣ | 6♦ | 6♣ | J♣ | A♦ | 7♥ | J♠ |

It's two pair, aces-up; the third pair has no standing.

| K♠ | Q♠ | 2♣ | Q♥ | J♠ | J♣ | Q♦ |

Full house.

| Q♥ | K♥ | 10♠ | 9♥ | 9♠ | A♥ | J♥ |

You must recognize that there is a flush mixed up in this straight.

| 6♥ | J♦ | 7♦ | 9♦ | 10♦ | Q♥ | 5♥ |

Queen-high bust.

| 3♣ | 7♣ | J♥ | 4♣ | 9♣ | 6♣ | 5♣ |

Straight flush.

betting

Bet on trips; bet or raise with a pat hand; check and call for less. Reraise with a full house or high flush when you think the competition is inferior. But, again, never do anything contrary to your best judgment simply because a rule exists. These are rules of thumb. The course of a hand will often disclose strong clues to an observant player.

Play of the game

On a separate sheet of paper, indicate with **fold, check, call, bet,** or **raise,** as you think best. (The game notation will not always show every fold or call by players who follow you in the betting order, as their actions have no effect on your own decision. Naturally, any opening bet or raise will have to appear, along with your reaction to the new terms of the wager.)

FIRST GAME

You	Vinnie	Emma	Marv	Lefty	Roxy	Silvio	Claire
6♥ 7♥ J♥	Q♠	J♠	Q♥	10♣	5♥	2♣	4♠
	bet	fold	fold	call	call	call	call
call							
3♥	3♣			9♣		5♦	6♠
	bet			call		call	call
raise							

A raise is best. A common strategy is to raise on the fourth card when you hold four in the same suit. Inasmuch as the odds for the flush are 40% in these circumstances, the bet is a good one. (You may bet a four-card sequence in the same way, but the odds are slightly less, and the hand is not as certain a winner as a flush.) Abandon this course if more than two of your suit are visible in other hands.

You	Vinnie	Emma	Marv	Lefty	Roxy	Silvio	Claire
7♦	J♦					4♣	
	check					check	
bet							

There are still two players left, and you are committed to drawing for the flush—if you do not play this kind of hand consistently, you may lose money over the long haul through betting unevenly. **Should you have bet against only one player remaining?** *Sure, you have signed on for the whole hand as of the fourth card. That is, you are committed to taking three more cards at 40% odds on the whole package—they're good odds.*

You	Vinnie	Emma	Marv	Lefty	Roxy	Silvio	Claire
9♥	A♠					6♦	
	check					bet	
raise	(fold)						

You may call, but a raise is more perspicacious, since Silvio can't have more than a straight at this point. It was a little foolish of him to bet at all—perhaps he chose this uneconomical means to test for your flush.

3♢							
bet							

You bet and win against the straight, and Silvio, who promised himself he would fold if you showed any sign of having the flush, has called anyway so that he could be sure. But mixing his tactics has cost him money.

SECOND GAME

You	Vinnie	Emma	Marv	Lefty	Roxy	Silvio	Claire
6♠ 9♠ 4♠	K♥	10♦	A♣	7♦	3♠	2♥	K♦
			bet	fold	fold	call	fold
call							
Q♠	J♣	10♣	6♣			5♦	
		bet	raise			call	
call							
Marv has preempted your raise on the prospects of a flush.							
10♠	9♦	10♥	3♣			J♥	
		bet	call			fold	
fold							

It's hard to fold a textbook flush, but Emma has, or is likely to complete, a full house; and Marv must have made his ace flush. (The mere fact that Marv has chosen to stay against the three bare-faced tens is persuasive, but coupled with his previous raise, it is undeniable.)

THIRD GAME

You	Vinnie	Emma	Marv	Lefty	Roxy	Silvio	Claire
A♢ 6♢ K♠	9♠	8♥	Q♠	6♥	A♥	10♦	9♥
					bet	fold	fold
call							
A♣		7♣	2♥		K♦		
					bet		
call							
4♥		6♠	4♣		3♠		
check							
Check to Emma's possible straight.							
		bet	call		call		
call							
6♣		10♣	2♠		5♠		
			check		check		
check							
Two good pair is a hand to stay with, not good enough for betting into a straight. And Emma checks too; don't be put off your guard—she may be sleeping on the straight.							
8♢							
			check		check		
check							
Check; likewise Emma. Yours is the best two pair and the best hand—this time.							

FOURTH GAME

You	Vinnie	Emma	Marv	Lefty	Roxy	Silvio	Claire
J♡ 9◇ 10♦	A♣	8♥	3♦	K♣	K♠	3♥	7♣
	bet	call	fold	fold	call	call	fold
call							
7♦	Q♠	9♣			6♥	J♣	
	check	check			bet	call	
call							

You're not betting an inside straight; you have figured that three draws remaining to possibilities *both* of a straight and a flush are worth the risk. Fair enough. Normally, you would fold in the fourth round with only three to the straight or the flush; combined, they add up to about 24% risk, which is acceptable.

K♥	2♠				4♠	10♣	
	check				bet	call	
call							

Now you have hopes for two inside straights. This does add up to the same thing as playing for a legitimate two-ended straight; that is, either one of two different cards (in this case any eight or queen) will complete your hand.

J♦	A♥				7♥	10♥	
	check				bet	call	
call							
Q♧	check				bet	raise	
call							

A straight isn't good enough to raise the raiser. Your straight beat Roxy's straight, but not Silvio's flush.

FIFTH GAME

You	Vinnie	Emma	Marv	Lefty	Roxy	Silvio	Claire
10◇ 4◇ 10♥	J♣	3♦	7♠	A♣	A♥	9♦	Q♦
				check	check	check	bet
call							
4♠	10♣			6♠	J♦	8♠	4♥
					check	check	bet
raise							

Raise or get out. The chief problem in drawing to one middling pair is precisely this: you may well make two middling pair. Now what? You must raise—to chase out a few of the uncertain hands—or fold, now. No amount of judicious discussion will solve the problem; it's a matter of taste and temperament. There is little doubt that you hold the best hand as of this round. Your chances for a full house, however, are significantly impaired by the exposed **10♣** and **4♥**.

You	Vinnie	Emma	Marv	Lefty	Roxy	Silvio	Claire
K♦							Q♣
							bet
fold							

Your raise pushed no less than four players out of the game. All these fireworks have gone for naught: Claire has drawn a queen and bet into the raiser. Three queens, queens-up? It doesn't matter; you are decidedly second best and likely to remain so.

SIXTH GAME

You	Vinnie	Emma	Marv	Lefty	Roxy	Silvio	Claire
K♣ 6♠ K♦	6♣	J♠	K♠	2♣	J♦	A♦	9♥
						bet	call
call							

6♦		10♥				7♥	3♥
						bet	raise
call							

If you wish to reraise on the basis of your early two pair, remember the odds for a full house out of this situation are fair—20%—but not good enough to reraise anyone.
Why did Claire raise?
Probably she has four hearts, but perhaps she is setting up a bluff.

10♠		4♣				8♦	4♥
						check	bet
call							

Claire may now have the flush; you can only hold on as inexpensively as possible, hope she is bluffing, and draw to the full house.

8♠		9♣					A♣
							bet
call							

Stay, of course; no real decision here.

9♤							
							check
check							

Should you bet? No. There is no use in stretching a good two pair farther than it will go. I suspect Emma would just raise you; she has stayed so quietly up to this point that I think it probable she is holding three of a kind, or, more likely, she made her straight on the last card. Call her bet, at any rate, unless you have never known Emma to come up short on the showdown.

SEVENTH GAME

You	Vinnie	Emma	Marv	Lefty	Roxy	Silvio	Claire
10♥ 2♥ J♥	4♦	2♠	9♠	A♣	6♥	K♦	A♠
				check	check	bet	fold
call							
J♠	Q♦	8♠				4♥	9♣
							bet
fold							

Don't stay for a middling hand just because the opportunity arises out of your blunted expectations of the flush. Even jacks-up, if you should be so lucky, is not likely a winner.

Let us repeat here that what you want is the best chance *from the outset* to outdraw the table, not a one- or two-card chance at a tardy miracle. Such miracles occur—and even playing conservatively you will sometimes need them—but not often enough to balance your outlays.

EIGHTH GAME

You	Vinnie	Emma	Marv	Lefty	Roxy	Silvio	Claire
J♣ J♦ J♥	3♦	Q♠	A♠	4♦	10♥	10♦	K♣
			check	check	check	check	bet
call							

Although a raise is certainly justified, delay it one round. Through no fault of your own, you are playing into a pretty desultory hand; a raise might drive out some weak cards who are willing, at Claire's price, to stay for one more card.

8♥	A♣	9♣			A♥		9♠
					check		bet
raise							

Now you must make the remaining players pay if they wish to stay and draw to straights and flushes.

6♣		6♥			5♦		8♣
					check		check
bet							

Don't ease up until raised or beat in sight.

4♥		Q♣			3♣		K♠
							check
bet							
6◇							
							check
bet		fold			raise		fold
reraise							

You recall, no doubt, that two aces have been folded. If Roxy has a full house, it can be no higher than tens-full; if she has an ace flush, we can only assume she raised because the possibility of your completely concealed boat has eluded her. (It's no shortcoming on Claire's part—a concealed boat just can't be diagnosed before money has changed hands in the seventh round.)

NINTH GAME

You	Vinnie	Emma	Marv	Lefty	Roxy	Silvio	Claire
A♦ 3♡ 3♦	10♥	A♣	4♠	Q♦	J♣	J♦	8♥
		bet	fold	call	fold	fold	call
call							

A very loose call.

3♣	9♠	A♥		2♦			5♦
		bet		fold			call
raise							

Raise or call. A raise is best because these are an unexciting set of trips, and your odds to win increase with every decrease in the number of active hands.

J♠	3♠	Q♣					
		check					
bet							

Your hand looks better against just two remaining players.

7♠	4♥	7♥					
		check					
bet							
2♡							
		check					
check							

Don't bet out on the last card. You have no information about the hole cards just dealt, and only a squeaky bunch of treys to show. Your trips win against aces-up and a busted straight.

seven-card stud low

Players compete for the lowest hand as in other forms of low poker.

strategy

In seven-card stud low, play for a seven-low or better. Because each additional card may bring you an unwanted pair, you should stay if your first four cards don't exceed a seven-low and then stay for the whole hand. If you have paid attention to exposed cards and betting habits of your opponents, you may occasionally bet a smooth nine- or eight-low with confidence.

As in seven-card stud (high), raise no later than the fourth card if you wish to drive out other hands.

This is, on the whole, a dull variant and not overly popular. When the game is dealt, participate only to the extent that your cards permit; that is to say, play this game as conservatively as you know how.

seven-card stud high-low

Pots are split between highest and lowest hands. An ideal low hand may win both ends of the pot. (An ideal low hand is one that may be counted both low and high: for example, a low flush, or one that can be arranged from the seven cards in two ways, one low combination and one high.)

There are two principal forms of seven-card stud high-low: a variant in which hands are simply compared at the showdown to find the winners, and a second variant, called declaratory high-low, in which players must express an intent to win either high or low, or both. No one who declares high, for example, can win the low end even if his is the lowest surviving hand; the low pot goes instead to the lowest of those hands that declared low.

The high-low declaration takes place after the seventh-card round of betting. Players take two chips in hand, and bring a fist from under the table containing none, one, or two chips. Usually, no chip indicates a declaration for the low end, one signifies the high end, and two are for both ends at once. To avoid unfair play, declarers should open their fists on a prearranged signal from the dealer. An extra round of betting may follow the declaration, but only if called for in the house rules.

(There is a third, or "sequential" declaration, variant of this game, in which players declare their intentions in turn starting with the high exposed hand or last raiser and proceeding to the left. Because this method puts the initial declarers at such a disadvantage, it is not recommended play. After all, the cards are quite arbitrary enough without passing out special favors to a few players at one end of the table.)

The "nondeclaratory," or "self-declaring," game requires no extra treatment, so we will be concerned here with the new wrinkles in declaratory high-low.

strategy

1. Stay only for a legitimate chance at either the high or the low end.
2. If, late in the game, the deal hasn't been as helpful as it might, look around—all may not yet be lost. While you were going for a low hand, did your exposed cards scare other potential low hands out of the pot? If so, stay; you will be the only player declaring low and thus a winner. The same thing, though somewhat more rarely, can happen while reaching for the high end. And it may happen that a potential high hand—such as a busted low flush—will suit you admirably for a low win.
3. If, by whatever prudent path, you arrive at a three-player declaration, one of you is to be an uncontested winner—the arithmetic is unavoidable—barring the somewhat rare eventuality of a two-way winner. This is the central problem, and the great attraction, of the game.

Which end will the other two players choose? If you can correctly divine from the cards on the table which way they will go, you may have the opportunity to declare as sole claimant to one end of the pot—even when your cards are far from deserving. Of course, they may well declare for the high and low ends respectively, leaving you with a middling loser. You will have to become practiced in the end-game speculation peculiar to this variant.

4. Don't declare both ways unless you are positive that both hands (you may assemble two different hands from your seven cards if necessary) are winners. *You must win both high and low to win at all.*

playing for the high end?

It is often observed that a good high-low player should be interested only in playing for the low end, that it is defective thinking to aim at the high end, which can be beaten both by another, legitimately higher hand and by the occasional low flush or straight. This is unconditionally not true in declaratory high-low (where the penalty for an unsuccessful two-way bid is quite stiff) and is at least doubtful in the self-declaring variety.

True, low players complete the straight more often than high players because they do not fold low assortments with one or two inside gaps to the straight; additionally, they are more often able to wait for the occasional flush that is made in the last two cards. You would prefer to be sitting on a pat low hand, waiting with detached amusement to fill a low inside straight, but *ma foi!* Someone has got to win all those high pots—about 90 percent of them—that are not claimed by a two-way hand. A full house, flush, or straight is still very much a winning hand, especially since any straight or flush held by the low winner is apt to be lower than those you are drawing to.

In sum: yes, you play at perhaps a 10-percent disadvantage going high, but that doesn't mean you can't win money at it, particularly when some of the players at the table are convinced that the high end is unplayable. But be wary with anything less than a high straight.

Play of the game

What follows are seven-card high-low games; **fold, check, call, bet,** or **raise** as you see fit. In the seventh round, you will be asked additionally to indicate your intent to declare **high, low,** or **both.** Complicated game.

FIRST GAME

You	Vinnie	Emma	Marv	Lefty	Roxy	Silvio	Claire
3♣ 4♣ 7♠	10♥	J♣	3♠	5♦	K♠	J♦	9♠
					check	check	check
check	bet	fold	call	call	call	call	fold
call							
6♠	8♦		A♦	6♣	4♦	J♥	
						bet	
call							

Call; don't raise. There are too many low-lying hands yet to be heard from.

2♦	Q♣		A♣	9♣	10♠	7♣	
			bet	fold	call	call	
raise							

Your hand is made and lower than anything in sight.

K♥	3♥		5♣		K♣	7♥	
						check	
bet							

Silvio is looking at two exposed pairs higher than his highest pair, the jacks; hence he checks. He knew, also, that any bet will elicit a raise from you, and he doesn't wish to be pulled into an upwardly spiraling investment.

			raise		call	call	
call							

Marv is probably raising against your low but may have aces-up.

5♡							
						check	
check							

Wait for Marv.

			bet		call	call	
call							

high/low/both?

High. Marv may have a little wheel or a six-low—his recent betting behavior is consistent with either. Roxy and Silvio don't appear to have a full house or flush between them, so that your straight should compete high. In fact, Marv has a little wheel but makes the mistake of declaring both ways. You are the sole winner: no claimant to the low pot (Roxy and Silvio went high), and you have won the high end, which in this case becomes the whole pot. Remember, you must win both ways when you declare both ways, or win nothing at all.

SECOND GAME

You	Vinnie	Emma	Marv	Lefty	Roxy	Silvio	Claire
A♣ 3♡ 2♥	Q♠	2♠	7♦	A♠	Q♣	10♦	3♦
				bet	fold	call	call
call							
These are near-perfect cards; only an open-ended chance at the low straight could be better.							
J♣	10♣	8♣		6♠		J♦	5♦
				check		check	bet
call							
8♥	4♠	A♦		6♥		7♥	10♥
				bet		fold	call
call							
5♥	10♠	6♦		K♣			Q♥
	bet	raise		call			fold
call							
There is no way of knowing whether Emma has chosen to disregard your eight-five or really has it beaten.							
J♡							
	check	bet		call			
raise							
You have drawn a late flush and hold an adequate low.							
	reraise	call		call			
call							
high/low/both?							

Low. Until the moment Vinnie reraised, you were sure to declare both ways. Vinnie's sandbagging raise is formally equivalent to turning up all five of his spades on the spot. Your eight-five low wins in the other direction.

Note the circumstances here: a high player, Vinnie, was able to sandbag another high player, Lefty, with no fear of a profitless round of checking since he could depend on Emma (a previous raiser) to bet. If Lefty raised, indicating a full house, then Vinnie could have considered folding, losing no extra money in this round. If Lefty merely called Emma's bet, then Vinnie planned to raise. He has cleverly exploited one of the tactical nuances that arise in the play of actual hands.

Lefty is a victim of the fact that two essentially separate games are being played at the same table. His first call (but not his second) was forced from plain necessity to stay in the hand he thought was being played out by the low-enders.

THIRD GAME

You	Vinnie	Emma	Marv	Lefty	Roxy	Silvio	Claire
Q♡ 4♡ Q♦	9♣	J♠	3♣	4♦	Q♣	A♦	10♥
						bet	call
call							
5♠		8♥	9♦	6♣	K♦	4♣	J♥
						bet	call
call							
We're staying too long on a pair of queens. Nobody's perfect.							
10♠			9♠	10♦	5♥	A♣	8♣
						bet	call
fold							
But we don't wish to be stupid. This is it, the middling hand you wish to avoid. Your queens are beaten on the board, and you can hope for a ten-low at best.							

FOURTH GAME

You	Vinnie	Emma	Marv	Lefty	Roxy	Silvio	Claire
2♣ A♥ 6♥	7♣	A♠	3♠	K♣	10♠	Q♥	K♠
		bet	call	fold	call	call	fold
call							
3♦	9♣	4♠	5♠		10♥	10♦	
					check	check	
bet							
Assert your claim to the low end now.							
K♥	5♦	8♦	5♥		K♦	9♠	
					check	bet	
call							
4♥	8♣	Q♦	J♣			10♣	
						bet	
raise							
Force the high-end players to pay for their last card.							
J♥						check	
bet	raise					call	
reraise							
(high/low/both?)							

Reraise and declare both ways. The cards have thrust this pot upon you; holding both a six-four low and an ace-king flush, you can have no excuse for missing the two-way declaration. Vinnie's is a last-card club flush and Silvio, who has had a straight from the fifth card, feels cheated and hollow inside.

FIFTH GAME

You	Vinnie	Emma	Marv	Lefty	Roxy	Silvio	Claire
A♦ 10♦ A♣	J♠	6♦	9♦	K♥	3♠	9♥	4♦
bet							

It's too bad you are the opener; a raise here could have been useful.

5♣		8♥	4♣	A♠	7♦		Q♦
				check	bet		call
call							

J♣		10♥	5♠	K♦	2♣		10♣
				bet	raise		fold
reraise							

You must discover now whether Lefty can be run out of the hand. Perhaps he holds no more than the pair. Since you haven't bluffed a flush all night, it may work. (In view of the cards now showing around the table, you stand about a 39% chance of drawing aces-up or better, so it's not a pure bluff.)

Q♣			3♥		2♦		
					bet		
raise							

Four exposed, suited cards can serve you almost as well as the real thing. In the event that one of the two remaining low players blunders into a straight, you must leave them with no doubt that you have the club flush.

Q♡							
					bet		
raise							
high/low/both?							

Raise and declare high. Marv, who drew into a six-low on the last card, reraised. You, of course, chipped in the third and final raise, and split the pot.

SIXTH GAME

You	Vinnie	Emma	Marv	Lefty	Roxy	Silvio	Claire
A♧ K♧ 3♦	6♥	9♥	2♦	K♠	J♦	8♦	2♥
				bet	fold	fold	call
call							
5♥	J♣	7♠	8♠	10♣			K♥
				bet			call
call							
2♣	4♥	Q♠	7♣	10♥			K♦
							bet
raise							

You have four cards to a good low, and fortunately three of your best are visible. A raise at this point will force out the middling hands, who have stayed one card too long as it is.

A♠			6♠	3♥			5♦
							check
bet							

Claire, the apparent high hand, would not normally check to the apparent low hand—it is in her interest to drive up the betting for what she figures is her end of the pot—but you are threatening a low straight, which would deny Claire any part of the pot.

			raise	fold			call
reraise							

Reraise is best; call is okay. Ask yourself why Marv raised.

A♡							
							check
bet							

high/low/both?

Bet, and declare low. The only explanation of Marv's behavior is a straight, probably five-nine; thus you must bet to support your claim to the low end, despite your three aces. Claire believes in Marv's straight and folds—there is no reason why she should question *your* hand's legitimacy. You and Marv split the pot by agreement without a showdown. Marv made the offer; for you to have offered could have been disastrous: Marv might have diagnosed your phony low and declared both ways. Of course, you would have declared low anyway and won your half even with a showdown. You have won half a pot by dint of a careful raise and a fortunate assortment of exposed cards. And no one is the wiser.

hold 'em

hold 'em

Two cards are dealt face down to each player; the first round of betting begins at the dealer's left. No checking is allowed in this round—players either call the opening bet or fold. (This is referred to as a "pass-and-out" or "pass-out" game; that is, if you pass in the first round, you are out of the game.) One card is burnt (thrown away face down), and three cards are turned up all at the same time in the center of the table. These are shared, or "common," cards. They, and two more that follow, are used by all players in conjunction with their two unexposed cards to form a poker hand. The first three exposed cards are called the "flop." Betting again starts with the first remaining player to the dealer's left, but from this time to the end of the hand, checking is allowed. A burn card precedes each of the last two cards, and there is a round of betting after each is turned up and added to the flop. The best five-card poker hand wins.

(The burn cards are customary in any common-card game. It often happens in the deal, even unintentionally, that the top card on the deck is tipped or glimpsed by the dealer. The practice of burning the top card protects the identity of the next common card—an understandable safeguard in this game, where each common card has much greater significance than any single card dealt into a player's hand.)

odds

Odds are not the same as for seven-card stud: there are crucial differences in play of the hands. In this game you *must* study the flop for its potential in forming not just your own hand but everyone else's as well. If, for example, two cards to the flush turn up in the flop, you can be nearly certain that one among the eight players present now has four to a flush. In general, expect the following:

1. If there is an ace or king in the flop, then somewhere around the table is *at least* a pair of aces or kings.

2. For every exposed pair in the flop there is a matching third card in hiding.

3. Two-card straights and flushes have a third and fourth at the table, willing to gamble on turning up a fifth.

4. Should a hand develop in which there are two pair exposed, you must reckon on a full house at the showdown.

Your play will be determined in hold 'em not so much by the cards you hold as by your estimate of how closely they fulfill the highest potential of the common cards.

Do not be surprised at the stringent standards for winning at hold 'em—there are, after all, eight players working at improvements to the single hand in the center of the table.

Hold 'em quiz

You are asked to analyze the common cards in the example below and give an opinion as to what hand the potential winner will most likely hold. Three-, four-, and complete five-card flops are studied.

2♥ 6♣ 5♥ / 4♥

There may well be a straight in this assortment, but a flush is the right answer.

A♦ 9♠ A♣

You can count on three aces, and even that has a chance to improve in the next two cards.

6♣ 7♣ 7♦ / 9♥ / 6♦

Again the straight is possible, but it doesn't win you a prize: the winner is probably a full house—sixes full of sevens or sevens full of sixes, take your pick.

Q♠ 9♠ 3♠

This is practically a guaranteed spade flush even at this early stage of the game.

10♣ 7♣ A♦ / 7♥ / 2♦

Hard to call; three sevens is possible, aces-up is more likely. Since the second seven did not appear until the fourth card, anyone holding only a pair of sevens may well have folded before the fourth card was dealt.

10♥ Q♦ J♠

This time the straight is screamingly evident, and a highly probable outcome on the hand.

It would be completely misleading to present a table of frequencies of hands in hold 'em or to devise winning percentages for the various hands. You would not benefit from knowing how often a full house occurs or how often two pair win on the average because the winning result in each individual hand is so dependent on the nature of the flop. In other words, better information than long-run percentages is available to you for the play of each hand. (To a certain extent, this is true of any kind of poker: you wish to know more than what the averages can tell you about any given hand. In most games, this kind of specific information can only be gleaned, with a considerable margin of error, from the betting behavior or observed idiosyncrasies of the other players; in hold 'em you are privileged to see a lot farther into the cards.)

The percentages in Table 16 are relevant. They will give you an idea of how often you should stay before the flop and define your risk in staying after a favorable flop.

TABLE 16

Odds, in the first two cards, to have an opening hand:			
pair			6%
A x			14%
K x			14%
in suit and possible sequence			12%
Odds for a favorable flop when holding:			
pair	that becomes	two pair	16%
		three of a kind	11%
		full house	1%
		four of a kind	0.2%
two in suit	that becomes	four in suit	11%
		flush	1%
two in sequence	that becomes	four in sequence	13%
		straight	1%
A x	that becomes	any improvement with at least paired **A**s	17%
K x	that becomes	any improvement with at least paired **K**s	17%
A K	that becomes	at least paired **A**s or **K**s	30%

(continued)

Odds, in the last two cards of the flop, when holding:			
two pair	to make	full house	16%
		four of a kind	0.2%
three of a kind	to make	full house	28%
		four of a kind	4%
four in suit	to make	flush	35%
four in sequence (open-ended)	to make	straight	30%
four in sequence (inside)	to make	straight	17%

Do not start tattooing these odds to the palms of your hands; they merely form the basis for a playing strategy to be covered in the next few pages.

strategy

When to stay before the flop:

A K

A x   the higher "x" is, the better, but

K x   set your own standards

pair

two suited cards to a straight—you may stay even if your cards are not in sequence. There is no disadvantage at this stage to drawing at an inside straight, or even with two or three cards missing in the middle of the straight. But they must be of the same suit, and middling to high.

When to stay after the flop:

two pair—stay if your two pair includes the highest card in the flop, but stay anyway if yours is a "concealed" two pair, that is, if both your hole cards have been paired.

three of a kind

four to an outside straight

four to a queen flush or better—stay for a lesser

flush at your own judgment and peril.

full house—stay, of course, but is yours the best full house that is likely to be made of the cards? If there should be three of a kind in the common cards, do not expect, but be wary of, a possible four of a kind lying in wait.

A goodly number of hold 'em players will tell you they never fold before the flop. The argument runs something like this: "Until I see those next three cards, all the hands at the table are of equal value. Even if I'm holding an unsuited **7,2** (no possibility of a straight, virtually none for a winning flush) who's to say that a **7,7,2** or **2,2,2** or some such won't turn up in the flop?" That is true as far as it goes, but if you elect to stay only when suited and preferably when sequentially eligible for the straight, then there are approximately 20% more combinations in the flop that can help you out. Hence, it is a better bet.

And, of course, your odds improve comparatively when holding a wired pair to make two pair, trips, or a full house during the course of the hand. As against an unpaired opener, you are 30% more likely to make two pair, 37% more eligible for trips, and 70% closer to a full house.

Staying for the last two cards: you should not fold in the last two cards unless developments have dramatically cheapened your own holdings. This might arise, for instance, when you hold two good pair, but the last two cards have been of the same suit (there was innocuous single in the flop), and the player to your right is fairly buzzing with new life.

Strategy quiz

Will you stay and meet the opening bet or fold with these openers?

A♥ 2♦	Q♥ 8♥	K♦ K♠	6♣ 8♠
Stay.	*Stay.*	*Stay.*	*Fold.*

9♣ J♣	J♥ 4♦	8♠ 8♦	K♣ 9♠
Stay.	*Fold.*	*Stay.*	*Stay.*

3♠ 3♥

Stay, but you will really need trips in the flop.

9♦ 10♣

Fold, there is nothing special about this unsuited couple, even though they are in exact sequence.

3♥ 6♥

To fold is probably best. Even if you make the flush, it may well be the second-best flush. You would, therefore, not be undertaking to play the hand with a chance at two winning combinations, that is, a straight or good flush, which is the whole point of staying with two suited, sequential cards.

betting

Bet as little as possible before the flop, as much as possible on the fourth and fifth cards when you have an iron-clad, made hand. The bet after the flop is not a good place to show your strength and no place for heavy betting if your hand isn't already made, though you may wish to bluff at this point if you detect a loss of momentum around the table—but don't try it often.

Play of the game

These are simulated hold 'em hands. Pay close attention to developing combinations within the flop, and indicate your intentions to *fold, check, call, bet,* or *raise.*

FIRST GAME

You	Vinnie	Emma	Marv	Lefty	Roxy	Silvio	Claire
6♡ K♤							
							bet
call		call	call	call			
The flop: 7♥ 5♦ 8♠							
							bet
call							
You opened with the king; now you are playing for an outside straight.							
Fourth card: 4♠							
							check
bet		call	call				
Fifth card: 6♦							
							check
check							
Fortunes swing quickly in hold 'em. With a six now in the flop, any loose nine beats your straight. Emma and Marv check too; neither has a nine, but Marv does have a straight identical to yours. Split the pot.							

SECOND GAME

You	Vinnie	Emma	Marv	Lefty	Roxy	Silvio	Claire
K♣ 9♣							
				bet	fold	fold	call
call	call	call					

The flop: 6♣ 10♦ 8♣

What are the likely outcomes of this hand?
A straight or a club flush are equally likely outcomes.
How many of them can you make in one card?
Both—either a seven or any club.

You	Vinnie	Emma	Marv	Lefty	Roxy	Silvio	Claire
				check			bet
call	call	call					

Fourth card: 7♥

You	Vinnie	Emma	Marv	Lefty	Roxy	Silvio	Claire
				check			check
bet							

Bet; you have the straight.

Fifth card: 7♣

You	Vinnie	Emma	Marv	Lefty	Roxy	Silvio	Claire
				check			check
bet	raise	fold					
reraise							

This is a golden opportunity. Vinnie, who has a club flush to the jack, has diagnosed your straight, but walked into your flush.

You	Vinnie	Emma	Marv	Lefty	Roxy	Silvio	Claire
	reraise						call
call							

Although you would welcome the opportunity to raise, all three raises have been used. Vinnie should have been more cautious—his second raise is a gift. Claire had a jack-high straight and felt for some reason she had to stay. Another gift.

THIRD GAME

You	Vinnie	Emma	Marv	Lefty	Roxy	Silvio	Claire
9◊ J◊							
(you are the opener)							
bet		call	call				call
The flop: 4♥ 9♥ J♠							
bet		call	call				call
With two pair from the flop, you'll be in to the last card.							
Fourth card: 4♠							
bet		call	call				call
Fifth card: 6♥							
check							
You didn't draw the full house, and there is room now in the flop for a heart flush or trip fours.							
			bet	.			fold
call							
Marv has a heart flush (but it might have been jacks over fours).							

FOURTH GAME

You	Vinnie	Emma	Marv	Lefty	Roxy	Silvio	Claire
J♧ J♡		fold	bet	fold	call	call	fold
call							
The flop: A♦ 10♥ K♥							
			bet		call	call	
fold							
Stay, if you want, but playing a lonely pair against this flop is an authentic act of faith. **Why?** *You must infer from the flop that there are aces or kings around the table (you are beat before you start) and a routine possibility for the heart flush.*							

FIFTH GAME

You	Vinnie	Emma	Marv	Lefty	Roxy	Silvio	Claire
7♣ 7♦					bet	call	fold
call		call					
The flop: **6♦ 7♠ A♥**							
					bet	call	
call		call					
Fourth card: **3♥**							
					bet	call	
raise							
The flop doesn't hold many threats for your trips. You may also call at this point and save the raise for next time.							
Fifth card: **K♥**							
					check	check	
bet		call					
There is not a great chance of a heart flush since only one was present in the first three cards. Roxy's second-best hand is aces over sixes.							

SIXTH GAME

You	Vinnie	Emma	Marv	Lefty	Roxy	Silvio	Claire
K♤ 4♧							
			bet	fold	fold	fold	call
call		call					

The flop: 6♠ J♣ K♦

			check				check
bet							

The table folds up. This slender pot is yours. When no one has meshed particularly well with the flop, you foist the pot upon yourself with even the shallowest show of self-confidence.

SEVENTH GAME

You	Vinnie	Emma	Marv	Lefty	Roxy	Silvio	Claire
A♢ A♧							
	bet	fold	fold	call	call	fold	call
call							

The flop: 8♥ 4♥ A♥

	check			bet	call		fold
call							

Your aces don't add up to much against a probable heart flush, but you have a 28% chance at a full house.

Fourth card: 9♠

				bet	call		raise
call							

Claire waited one round to let everyone know she has the flush; Lefty may have another. You've paid for the last card—if it doesn't fill your boat, fold.

EIGHTH GAME

You	Vinnie	Emma	Marv	Lefty	Roxy	Silvio	Claire
5♣ 5♦							
			bet	fold	call	fold	call
call							
The flop: J♣ 8♣ J♥							
			bet		call		call
fold							

Habits formed in other kinds of poker make it hard to relinquish two pair, but a mere eight has you beat. This is a hazardous flop; the fact that three other players have stayed notwithstanding increases the likelihood of a third jack or even a big wired pair in their assortments.

hold 'em high-low (qualified-low hold 'em)

Hold 'em is rarely played as a strictly low game, but an interesting high-low variant exists: three hole cards (instead of the usual two) are dealt to each player; one is thrown away *after* the flop. A player, therefore, has looked at six cards before culling his hand. You and everyone else have handled enough cards by the second bet that you must count on even stiffer openers than in the game's two-card version. In this variant, no low hand higher than an eight is eligible for the low end of the pot—there is no split at all if no hand qualifies for the low end.

As with any high-low game, you must participate with a view to winning one end or the other, but this game is especially tricky for the low player. You are urged not to play for the low end with less than four low cards, one of which should be an ace (or, if the ace is a common card, a deuce).

It is just possible to play legitimately for both ends at once. A "wheel" or a low flush is generally enough to bring off this coup (straights and flushes are not recognized for the purposes of determining the low hand), or a high hand may be eked out of a rearrangement of the seven cards in play.

The chances of making a straight are particularly improved (see appendix 2.) in this game because six cards are examined all at one time.

Play of the game
Once again, remind yourself that each player looks at six cards before committing himself in earnest. No other non-wild game will produce high hands as frequently as this one. On a separate sheet of paper, select **fold, check, call, bet,** or **raise.**

FIRST GAME

You	Vinnie	Emma	Marv	Lefty	Roxy	Silvio	Claire
9♦ 7♥ 10♥							
		bet	fold	call	call	call	fold
call							
Uninspired cards; folding is not a bad idea. The pot promises to be large, however, so you may as well stay for the flop.							
The flop: A♠ J♥ 7♠							
Throw away _____? 7♥							
		check		bet	call	call	
fold							
Nothing but an inside straight—you needed an open-ended draw or four to the flush to consider staying.							

SECOND GAME

You	Vinnie	Emma	Marv	Lefty	Roxy	Silvio	Claire
A♣ 2♣ A♢							
					bet	call	fold
call							

This one of the best opening hands in qualified low hold 'em. You may opt for a good high or an unbeatable low depending on the flop. **A A 3, A K 2, A K 3, A 2 2, A 3 3** are all excellent openers. **A A 2** and **A A 3** are worth a raise in this initial round, if you wish.

The flop: 3♦ K♥ 9♦

Throw away _____?
2♣ You see only three cards to a low hand; you need four. Play for the high end.

You	Vinnie	Emma	Marv	Lefty	Roxy	Silvio	Claire
					check	check	
check		check	check				

Fourth card: 3♥

You	Vinnie	Emma	Marv	Lefty	Roxy	Silvio	Claire
					check	bet	
call							

It's now impossible that anyone is playing for the low end. Claire's bet may indicate an optimistic kings-up, or it may be trip threes.

Fifth card: 3♠

You	Vinnie	Emma	Marv	Lefty	Roxy	Silvio	Claire
					check	bet	
call							

From a promising start, this hand has developed some unwelcome features. You hold the best full house, and under normal circumstances you would bet accordingly. You must, however, anticipate the presence of the case three. Silvio has it, making four all together.

THIRD GAME

You	Vinnie	Emma	Marv	Lefty	Roxy	Silvio	Claire
8♡ 8◇ J◇							
			bet	fold	fold	call	call
call							

The flop: 6♣ 3♣ J♠

Throw away _____?
Either of the eights. Doesn't it make more sense to hold jacks than eights?

			check			bet	call
call		call					

Fourth card: 4♣

			check			bet	raise
call							

The betting action seems to belong to low-end hopefuls.

Fifth card: 6♥

			check			check	bet
call							

The high end belongs to you. Silvio shucked a paired six, arranging his cards for an optimum chance at the low hand.

FOURTH GAME

You	Vinnie	Emma	Marv	Lefty	Roxy	Silvio	Claire
2♣ 6♡ A♢							
					bet	call	call
call	call						

The flop: A♣ 5♥ 10♦

Throw away _____?
A♦ Playing for an excellent low is better than playing for an unclear high combination.
As the hand now stands, what two-card combinations would be lower than your own?
Only three of them—**3,2; 4,2;** and **4,3.**

Fourth card: Q♥

					check	check	bet
call	call						

Fifth card: 4♣

					check	check	bet
raise							

Now, only one combination, a **3,2,** could take the low end away from you. Your risk is negligible.

FIFTH GAME

You	Vinnie	Emma	Marv	Lefty	Roxy	Silvio	Claire
2♤ 9♤ 9♡							
						bet	call
call	call	call	fold	call	fold		

The flop: 8♣ 9♦ 6♠

Throw away _____?
2♠ Yes, there is a spade flush in the making, and it will be higher than your nine. Your best chance is with the trip nines.

						bet	fold
call	call	call					

Fourth card: Q♣

						bet	
call	raise	call				call	
call							

The flush hasn't made yet, the straight is a long shot, no guaranteed low hand—it's hard to know what Vinnie is banking on. Queens-up? Trip queens?

Fifth card: K♥

						check	
check							

You should respect Vinnie's raise. (This time he holds only queens-up. He believed, reasonably, everyone to be drawing at the straight or the flush.)

SIXTH GAME

You	Vinnie	Emma	Marv	Lefty	Roxy	Silvio	Claire
8♡ 6♣ 8♣							
				bet	call	call	fold
call							

Call, or fold. This hand could turn into a middling flush, a middling straight, a precarious low. You can justify staying for the flop in qualified low hold 'em on just about anything, but these are near the bottom.

The flop: 7♣ K♦ 9♥

Throw away _____?
8♥ Not the 8♣—it's a slim chance for the flush, but keeping the club instead of the heart costs you nothing.

				check	check	bet	
call							

Fourth card: 5♣

				check	check	check	
bet							

Now you hope the fifth club doesn't turn up. Your concealed straight has a stronger chance of winning than a low club flush, which is all you will have if another club falls into the flop.

Fifth card: K♠

				check	check	check	
Bet; and win.							

SEVENTH GAME

You	Vinnie	Emma	Marv	Lefty	Roxy	Silvio	Claire
A♤ 5♧ 3♧							
		bet	fold	fold	call	call	call
call							

The flop: 7♥ 9♥ 5♠

Throw away _____?
5♣ Don't hold a pair on the assumption you can decide later to go high or low. Mostly, you will be runner-up in both events.

		bet			fold	fold	call
call							

Fourth card: J♠

		bet					call
call							

Fifth card: A♥

		check					check
check							

Your low is busted. The aces lose to Emma's jacks-up. If you had kept the five, you would have won. There's nothing to be learned here except that good play only pays off on the average, not every time.

sleepers, grinders, rocks, & runners

Good players must vary their poker styles. Not infrequently you will encounter players without the flexibility to accomplish this. A few of them have built their games around a single, usually valid approach in which the only flaw is the witless predictability of style.

Just as it is gratifying to recognize a familiar period or style in music and art, it is profitable to be familiar with a few styles in poker. (Of course, no one is going to salute your critical discernment and aesthetic sense; you'll have to take your rewards out of the pot.) Learn to recognize the four people described below. A judicious adoption and mingling of these four strategies in your own game covers a lot of ground in poker, and you should experiment (as cheaply as possible) with them.

the rock

The rock is a safe player; always bets by the book (as indeed everyone should on balance)——a check means weakness or a long-shot in the making, a bet is for cautious possibilities, and a raise denotes the genuine article. The rock folds in all the right places and rarely wins big.

There are three problems with this method as an exclusive approach to winning. First, you can almost read the rock's cards from his betting behavior. Good players know when to drop out against him, and his best hands (which are the only ones he pursues) win him little money.

Second, the rock is easily bluffed. Because he himself draws all of his strength from his cards, he can be persuaded out of hands in which someone else is pointedly representing strength.

Third, and most damning, the rock plays his hand and his hand only. He does not pay enough attention to signals and developments around him. Good cards are not measured against a national standard but only against the other hands in any given poker episode.

The rock is the least deceptive of players.

the runner

The runner is in many ways the opposite of the rock. His play is founded on the principle that any hand can win, especially if the field is narrow or if he can scare most of the players out with heavy initial betting and ''run'' with his cards to the showdown. The runner may ease off in later betting, depending on his cards, or fold if his opening bet didn't sufficiently reduce the opposition.

Because the runner is as likely as anyone else to hold good opening cards, the strength of his system is in its inscrutability. It is impossible to know whether he is betting his cards or betting merely to reduce the number of hands in play against him. The obvious failing of an unswerving runner is consistency. Gradually, the number of players who will stay with him increases, his stake decreases.

the grinder

The grinder is fearsome. He sits quietly at his end of the table chewing on a splayed cigar until he receives the best of opening combinations. Then he wades into the pot with the maximum bet. All of his bets and raises will be for the maximum amount; playing with him can be very expensive if you haven't recognized the type.

His play is a conservative variation on the theme that best hand going in is best going out—his standards for entering the pot are the highest at the table; thus he stays less frequently and wins a good percentage of the time. He is the scourge of average players. Please note that the grinder seldom bluffs, but he has an excellent chance of bringing it off when he does.

The simple alternative to transferring your assets to a grinder is to let someone else play against him unless you too have blue-ribbon openers. When you have good and sufficient reason to stay against him, you too should bet and raise in increments of the maximum allowable.

the sleeper

The sleeper plays an average sort of game—deliberately—while waiting for his opening to develop. Specifically, he is waiting to hold the whip hand in a contest that is ostensibly between two or more praiseworthy but insufficient hands. The sleeper has merely to go along with the spirited raises that are enlarging *his* pot. When he weighs in with a surprise raise of his own in the final round, you can bet he is holding a complete set of the encyclopedia.

There is no flaw in playing as a sleeper so long as you confine it to an occasional demonstration; otherwise, by laying back, you may deny yourself in routine hands the bigger pots you might have built with more aggressive play.

Although truly windfall opportunities do develop for a sleeper, they are truly rare in less than a long evening of seven- to eight-handed play.

In conclusion, most people have no trouble, if they are adequately informed, in playing a safe, percentage game. But you can't win consistently in an average game or better if you don't deliberately foster some imponderables in the way your style is perceived. You must assume the guise of a runner, particularly, or a sleeper, or a grinder on occasion. Predictability can lose you almost as much as a string of second-best hands. The psychological attunement of your opposition will suffer all out of proportion to the actual variation in your play. You need add no more than 5 to 10% of premeditated confusion to your game for a significant result.

appendices

1. on theories of percentage play & the size of the pot

Theory 1 One sensible school of thinking proposes that it is not the object of a poker player to win pots that do not cover the risk he takes to win them. A player should, therefore, closely monitor the contents of the pot to know when the percentages have swung in his favor.

To illustrate, suppose you are drawing a final card to an outside straight—in five-card draw the odds to make it are 17%; you may expect over time to complete it approximately every sixth time you play this hand. We will imagine that each hand has cost you $10; to show a profit you must win back at least $50 on the sixth occasion, when the draw is good, to cover the $50 you lost in the five hands that didn't pan out.

The idea seems simple enough, but it lacks clarity in application. First, what are the appropriate odds? In our example, you know that the odds to succeed *in the draw* are 17%—but still you do not win if someone else has drawn the flush. Clearly 17%, the odds to draw, are not the same thing as the odds *to win*.

In actual play you must worry both about the chances of making the hand you want and the chance that your hand, once made, is the best at the table. This is, at best, an informed guess.

Second, how are the odds used to calculate betting behavior? Does a five-to-one chance mean that you can afford to lose exactly five times and recoup on the sixth? No. Depending on the game, you invest less in your unsuccessful draws than in the hands you play (presumably with good cards) right up to the showdown. With an unsuccessful draw, you would drop out before the final round of betting. Exact figures don't exist, but it is reasonable to assume that your outlays to pursue a draw, in relation to the cost of staying for a whole hand, do not exceed *40 to 50% in five-card draw* or approximately *80% in seven-card stud and hold 'em*. This means, as in our draw to the straight, that if you are losing $10 per luckless try, you will invest about $25 (10 is 40% of 25) in the pot when you have made the straight. Your winnings, thus, are in multiples of that $25 (multiply $25 by every competing player who stayed for the whole game or fraction thereof). So. You stand to win a little "faster" than you lose—a good thing, but remember we still haven't taken into account, nor can we with any precision, that your straight may lose to a higher hand. Please note that even with all eight players betting into your pot at the showdown (never happens), and equipped with a guarantee signed and sealed in heaven that your made hand will win (rarely happens), no odds less than 6% could possibly pay you back. The figure is about 11% for stud and hold 'em. And these are the most optimistic figures possible—you should double them for use in the real world. The resulting numbers— 12% and 22%, give or take a few percentage points— are the bottom line for sound betting practice in limit poker.

Note also that these figures tell the complete and unexpurgated history of drawing to straights and flushes, but diminish in importance for other types of draw. Whereas a good pair may improve to two pair or three of a kind, which are good hands in themselves and capable of further improvement, the fragmentary straight or flush can easily turn into nothing at all; you may be strapped even to produce a weak pair by the showdown.

In this book, you have been advised from time to time to stay for a thin draw on the basis of the probable minimum size of the pot. No attempt has been made to count the pot and divide by some magic number. The examples all include a cushion adequate to cover good draws that lose in the showdown. Scrupulous counting of the pot and lots of long division do not somehow make your game more "scientific." Approximate thresholds, with room for the uncertainties involved, are about the best that can be obtained.

Theory 2 Don't play for a two-man pot? This poker tenet
holds that you must avoid playing in slender pots, against
a single opponent, for instance. If you have entered a
hand with promising cards, and stay on the right premises,
you have at least a 50% chance of winning, or in the
adage of poker: *The best hand going in has the best
chance to win.* And if you did win only 50% of the time,
you still show a profit because of any force-bets or antes in
your share of pots. No hand should be folded prematurely
because of an imagined disadvantage in playing two-
handed. Obviously, you shouldn't begin a head-to-head
contest holding three cards to a straight or flush (in seven-
card stud) or four cards to the same (in five-card draw). It is
madness to play these openers unless five players and
yourself stay in the first round. This preserves a winning
margin even with two players folding in subsequent
rounds. (Four other players starting is good enough if you
think you can count on at least two of them to stay for the
showdown.)

2. the trouble with straights

Many experienced seven-card stud players develop suspicions about the straight: it doesn't seem to turn up as often as it should; the flush seems an easier hand to make. Can this be? Is poker mistaken in assigning the straight a relatively more common rank than the flush?

In fact, as we shall see, there is something skewed in the occurrence of straights, although it is theoretically a more frequent hand than the flush, and no mistake was made in arranging the values of poker hands.

To begin with, no one plays every hand to the last card. Depending on your instinct and education in these matters, you will drop out of all but 5 to 20% of hands you are dealt. Most players, in theory at least, recognize the same indications and standards for staying and for folding as a hand develops. Hands that fate ordains will have to be made in the last two turns of a card are rarely still in play. Hence, not every flush, or straight, or four of a kind is allowed to occur. Players fold, for example, about 40% of the hands that would have been flushes—even taking into account those cases in which a good two pair or three of a kind turns into flushes in the last cards.

There is no reason to despair of carelessly donating these hands to the Great Void; you would lose money at a championship rate if you attempted to stay for all the remote possibilities in your cards. Also, nothing fundamental is upset by this state of affairs: you and everyone else will throw away nearly the same percentages of four-of-a-kind, full-house, flush, and three-of-a-kind hands. But not straights.

The trouble with straights is the guidelines most players use, correctly, to draw them. A straight can be dealt, card by card as in seven-card stud, 2,520 ways (and that's without regard to permutations of suit, which are irrelevant in all but the rare event of a straight flush). About 40% should be folded, like the flush, at the fifth card or earlier. Because an additional 15% of completed straights would have to develop from one-, two-, or even three-card gaps to an inside straight, there is an extra impediment to making the straight. (You should appreciate by now why the inside straight is an impediment to every right-thinking poker player.) In other words, the exact order in which your straight is dealt has crucial significance to your strategy. No similar problem exists with other types of hands: you do not concern yourself, for instance, with the order in which your flush turns up, only with the raw number of cards in suit.

More complications arise. When drawing to a four-card outside straight or to a four-card flush, the odds actually favor the supposedly more difficult flush. Once again the straight does not seem to perform up to advertised specifications. You must remember that the value of poker hands is calculated on the basis of all combinations that could be dealt. The shortcoming of the straight against this expectation results strictly from the methodology of playing for the straight. It is true that a four-card flush is easier to fill, but it does not occur as frequently as four cards to a straight.

As practical evidence of these remarks, you may notice how much more often a straight is made in seven-card high-low games than in strictly high games. This is because low-end players may hold assortments of low cards with gaps they could not profitably hope to fill in high poker, but which occasionally turn into the less probable missing straights.

In sum, don't mistrust the straight (except when you think you're beat), but don't take miscalculated plunges with the idea that somehow you are not making some of the straights to which you are "entitled."

3. etiquette

1. Always bet and fold in turn. No one wants to deny you the chance to tip off your hand prematurely, but the play of others may be compromised by overeager actions on your part.

2. Don't try to make conversation with players engaged in a hand when you are not.

3. Ante without being reminded. The evening passes very slowly if a permanent Inquisition must be installed to keep track of late antes.

4. Most players object to being watched over the shoulder; assume this to be the case. (Kibitzers may unwittingly register a telling emotion while watching a hand develop.)

5. Don't handle the cards so roughly as to leave them crimped. For one thing, your clumsiness is apt to be misconstrued.

6. By all means count your chips as often as you wish; just don't do it out loud.

7. Don't touch the deadwood. (Deadwood is discarded hands.)

8. Guard your hand closely—it's your responsibility completely. Other players will be only slightly embarrassed to take your money when you expose cards.

9. In a game among friends, it is "polite" for winners to announce their intention to leave somewhat ahead of time. Or you may simply nurse your winnings through the rest of the evening. When playing in a public game, a casino game, leave at any time you wish.

10. Lastly, win and lose with perfect grace. Although this is impossible in practice—no one possesses a perfect indifference to the vicissitudes of play—it is a noble thought and should appear in print as often as possible.

4. wild-card games

The addition of wild cards, extra cards, optional cards, and so on to a poker game invariably shifts the odds— sometimes in subtle ways. Advantages accrue to those who study the games most thoroughly. Unless you have prepared yourself in the specifics of a few wild games (there are innumerable variations) or unless you are gambling with like-minded adventurers for throw-away stakes, don't play. The sheer number of these extra-dimensional forms restricts their popularity. And many players feel that the drama and psychological finesse of the game suffer with the introduction of wild cards.

variations, aberrations, deviations, and real perversions

There can never be a complete listing of all the gadgets, gimmicks, novelties, and wild-card games played in the poker world. Here is a brief description of a few most frequently encountered games:

variations arising out of five-card draw

Shotgun Played and dealt as five-card draw but with betting rounds after the third, fourth, and fifth cards of the deal.

Spit-in-the-ocean Four cards are dealt face down to each player; a fifth is turned up in the center of the table. The common card, or "widow," is wild, as are the remaining three of its kind. The widow may be turned up at any time during the deal, either at the dealer's discretion or at any player's calling the word "spit."

Wild cards The wild cards most usually called in five-card draw (and often tacked onto seven-card stud games) are deuces, one-eyed jacks, or a single joker. I have never seen two jokers used in a poker game and can't account for this singular, righteous omission among all the improbable novelties into which players will freely throw their money. Five-of-a-kind outranks every other hand in wild-card poker.

aberrations of five-card stud

Canadian or New York stud In this game a four-flush beats one pair but not two pair.

Indian poker Whenever you see what appears to be an excited knot of mentalists with cards pressed to their temples, you have probably run across an outlandish variant of poker. Players may not look at the hole card in their own hands. Instead, it is held face outward at the forehead for the duration of the game. This means that every player will have a perfect knowledge of all the hands at the table except his own—an exact inversion of the usual circumstances of poker.

Mexican stud The first two cards are dealt face down; each player turns up one card of his own choosing ("roll your own"). The third, fourth, and fifth cards are likewise dealt face down in each subsequent round, and one card is rolled before the betting commences. (Anyone wishing to become embroiled in the floating wild-card variant of Mexican stud known as Shifting Sands would do well to study A. D. Livingston's excellent commentary on the game in *Poker Strategy and Winning Play,* Hollywood: Wilshire, 1971. No wild-card game better illustrates the subtlety of advantage that accrues to a prepared player.)

Shucks or option cards Stud games are sometimes dealt with an option to shuck, or throw away, a card and receive a new one in its place. Exercising the privilege generally costs an amount that is announced before the hand.

Six-card stud Dealt as five-card stud but with a sixth, face-down card and additional round of betting.

deviations from seven-card stud

Some games with simple wild cards added:

Betty Hutton Nines and fives are wild.

Dr. Pepper Tens, twos, and fours are wild.

Heinz Fives and sevens are wild.

Woolworth Fives and tens are wild.

Baseball Nines and treys are wild, but with the proviso that any face-up trey must pay the pot (in some games, match the pot) to stay in the game. The trey is both a wild card and a risk. An additional, face-down card is dealt every recipient of a four. "Football" is just like "Baseball" but with sixes, fours, and twos serving respectively in the places of nines, treys, and fours.

Chicago The high spade in the hole (face down) splits the pot with the high hand. Sometimes a "low Chicago," or low spade split, is called instead.

Low hole card wild Lowest face-down card and all like it are wild. Hence, the advent of the seventh card may completely derange a hand by changing the wild card's denomination.

real perversions

Anaconda, a.k.a. Screwy Louey Seven cards dealt face down, three cards are passed to the player on the left. All players then throw away two cards and prepare to roll their own best five-card hand with a round of betting before each flip. Very slow game.

Cincinnatti, a.k.a. Lamebrain, Tennessee Five cards are dealt face down to each player and a five-card, face-down widow in the center. Betting commences at the end of the deal, with further rounds as the common cards are turned up one by one.

Crisscross Five cards are dealt face down to each player; five visible widow cards are dealt one by one into a cross-shaped pattern—a vertical and horizontal row of three cards each, intersecting at the center card. The card at the center of the widow is always dealt last. Players may utilize cards from either row of the cross, but not both, to form a best hand. Betting begins before the first widow card is dealt and resumes with each new common card. "Southern Cross" is played much the same but with a larger widow; this game employs nine common cards in two intersecting rows of five cards each.

No peek Seven cards dealt face down, no player may look at his cards. Instead, the age turns up his top card and opens the betting. The next player must roll his cards until he beats the first player's exposed card, and each successive player turns his cards until he beats the best showing at the table or exhausts his hand. There is a round of betting after every player turn.

5. cheating & unusual play

As long as you confine your poker playing to public games and gatherings of acquaintances, you will encounter little or no cheating. The fabled "mechanic" is exceedingly rare—his skills take years of dedicated practice—and nearly undetectable by players who are not looking, and listening, for the marks of his craft. You are more likely to encounter the pedestrian varieties of petty cheating, some of which are not even undertaken with a fully conscious intent.

If a player has demonstrated a tendency to throw less than the full amount into the pot, you will work yourself into a bleary frenzy trying to keep track of him. Don't play in games that he attends.

Play with a new, sealed pack of cards. (Yes, new, sealed, marked decks are available; I'm hoping you don't know anyone who would use one.) If you wish, subject the deck to the "moving picture" test. Holding the deck securely in one hand, riffle the cards with your free thumb. Study the backs of the cards. Does anything appear to move? Do this several times, looking at different areas of the design. If the design is undoctored, it is identical on every card and nothing moves. If something has been added or subtracted, the design will appear to move or jump, as in a crude cartoon. Any crimping or scratching of the cards during play is grounds for calling for a new deck.

Insist that the elementary poker safeguards be scrupulously observed when you play:

> Cards may never disappear below the level of the table.
> A clearly audible, verbal intent to bet is binding.
> String bets are not allowed.
> Hands should be kept off the deadwood.
> If you find that the dealer cannot keep the bottom card concealed, insist that the deck be covered at the bottom.

As I have said, much cheating occurs without planned intent. Ensure that your hand is not being tipped by any mirrors or reflective surfaces around the room. Discourage kibitzers who observe your hand from behind. *And guard your own cards.*

Occasionally, two or more players combine, through a system of signals, to enrich those pots they figure to win. Players can sometimes be steered by the active bust into a quiescent "sleeper." It's not a windfall technique, but it can be effective enough. If you suspect that this or any other overt kind of cheating is taking place, leave the game.

side bets

In some games, depending on the house rules, players are allowed to place a "side bet" with any takers on any issue of interest in a particular hand. A situation may be permitted to arise, therefore, in which two different games are being played out within the same hand. For example: suppose that a group of four players at the table (out of the eight who are present) decide they will place a separate wager on the best hand among the four of them. No problem? Far from it; if the side bets are large enough, these four players will stay for the showdown in nearly every case, just to compete for the side pot. Often enough, they will make winning draws to hands they would have folded when playing strictly for the main pot. Thus, if you are not participating in the side pot arrangement, you play at a twofold disadvantage. First, you cannot count on driving out weak hands—they will stay regardless of what you have, if they think they are still competitive within the side pot. Second, you will lose more frequently than you otherwise would because these entrenched weak hands can turn into winners when allowed to stay and draw, and will end up with your pot as well as the side bets.

An occasional side bet—on the turn of a particular card, perhaps—is exciting, but be warned if you play in games in which the side-betting is systematic and more or less continual.

6. playing in Las Vegas

There is a hole in every Las Vegas poker table; through it fall several hundred thousands of dollars each year, and some of it might be yours. This fact needn't deter you from playing the game. After all, the proprietors of those casinos provide you with a secure, completely honest, and continuous opportunity to play poker. Be sure, however, that you understand the mechanics of a typical house cut before you sit down in one of those comfortable chairs. Two systems are in use:

1. The house may deduct a percentage from the pot as a hand develops. For example, a sign over the seven-card stud table may give notice, in a $1–$3 game, that 5% but not exceeding $3 is extracted from each pot. Well, a pot without a name on it is a fairly impersonal and even somewhat abstruse concept, and the house is a simple 5% partner in its division. Please note that the house has never thrown any chips into a pot and that its share, therefore, is unadulterated profit. As soon as a pot has a name on it, like your own name if you wish, the house's share can become as much as 10% of your *winnings*. This is not sleight of hand. The house must calculate its "rake" on the basis of all the chips on the table; you must calculate your winnings from the chips in excess of what you put into the pot. If you have wagered $10, and other contributions amount to $30, then $40 is at stake; 5% of $40, or $2, is owed the house, but there were only $30 of winnings in the pot and the house has taken $2 of that. $2 is 6.7% of $30. You should understand what is happening here: what the house calculates as a percentage of the entire pot you are obliged to compute as a percentage of a smaller amount, your actual winnings. Assuming that you lost 6.7% of winnings to the house on every pot (this is only a typical figure, the actual percentage varies inversely as the number of people in a particular pot), you would have to play at least 6.7% better than average just to break even. Perhaps you will play well enough to soak up these odds, but nonetheless it does take the snap and pace out of winning.

Don't forget to take into account your tip to the dealer after winning—that comes out of your winnings too.

2. Particularly in higher stakes games, fixed charges may be levied on each player, either as seat rentals, collected at regular intervals, or as antes before each hand. As a rule, these will amount to a smaller bite of your winnings than a straight percentage rake. House percentages or fixed rates, tips, and force bets insure that you will rarely play at less than a steady 10% disadvantage.

In view of the foregoing, it is wise to avoid entrenching yourself for any length of time in a game in which you are making no real headway against the table. When more or less equal players, more or less equally favored by the cards, sit for a spell at a casino table, all their stakes evaporate at a more or less equal rate. It may be educational, but such a session produces no winners. The casinos provide poker on demand, at any hour, every day of the year; leave a game in which you feel you are matched or beaten.

Do not fret about the occasional presence of shills (house players) in the casino games. At least, don't fret for the wrong reasons: shills do tend to impede the flow and action of the game; if the house can't round up some bonafide players within a reasonable time, you should consider shifting your ground. Shills sit only at tables with a temporary shortage of players, and they are not actively trying to hustle your money. For one thing, they are not allowed to put the house's money at risk in any sort of imaginative play. By the same token, neither should you put your money at risk against a shill whose cards have met the boss's inflexible standards for extended betting. Shills are happy (and required) to identify themselves when asked. Bet into a shill only when you *know* yours are better cards.

No one can count on winning in Las Vegas, you will have done well to play and leave town with a good deal of your original stake intact. There are winners, of course; they are usually the better players—an unusual result among other casino games.

7. laws: the California myth

The Supreme Court of California and that state's legislature have been much maligned of late in oral and printed traditions. Singly or in concert, it is often asserted, they have promulgated the statutory notion that draw poker—legal in California by restricted local option—is a game of skill, stud poker a game of chance. Judges and politicians are no more susceptible of the truth than you or I, but could they have strayed so far from it in their counsels?

They have not. California law provides that:

Every person who deals, plays, or carries on . . . any game of faro, monte, roulette, lansquenet, rouge et noire, rondo, tan, fan-tan, stud-horse poker, seven-and-a-half, twenty-one, hokey-pokey, or any banking or percentage game played with cards, dice, or any device, for money, checks, credit, or other representative of value . . . is guilty of a misdemeanor. . . . (§330 Cal. Pen. Code.)

Draw poker is legal in California by its explicit and intentional absence from this list of prohibited games. (The list, by the way, was drawn up in 1872 and lengthened in 1885 and 1891; we can't accuse the California legislature of not doing its homework.) The courts, however, have never maintained that draw poker is distinguished from stud in any way other than its legality. From its earliest decision—a decision that is still quoted as precedent in these matters—the court has said:

Poker, played for money, however objectionable in fact, is, in the eyes of the law, as innocent as chess, or any game played for simple recreation. . . . (*Ex Parte Meyer*, 40 P. 953 at 954. 1895.)

In an important, later case it is stated more plainly: "Draw poker is assuredly a game of chance or, in other words, gambling." (*Lavick v. Nitzberg*, 188 P.2d 758 at 759. 1948).

As to why the California legislature may have acted as it did to exempt draw poker from the penalties of law, especially in the recent licensing of gaming houses (the "Gardena clubs"), we may refer to *Carrier v. Brannan,* 3 Cal. 328 at 329:

The legislature, finding a thirst for play so universally prevalent throughout the State, and despairing of suppressing it entirely, have attempted to control it within certain bounds. . . .

We see that in California, as in most other states, the authorities are not so much interested in a determination of skill or chance in a game but more in the mere fact of gambling. They object not so much to the hazards involved as to a perceived public immorality; they wish, if possible, to protect the populace from its own unfettered greed and, more particularly, from those who operate these games for profit. I believe that any legal theory based on proportionality of skill and chance in a money game is now dated, and has never really been more than a secondary, tactical argument in the considerations of the courts. (For a contrary view, but written some fifty years ago, the reader may consult 23 Vir. Law Rev. 431.)

Anyone still inclined to appeal to the bench for the last word in this matter should sit down in a wise jurisdiction and play seven-card stud with a few judges.

8. real-time experimentation

The following are ideas familiar to most poker players, and you may wish to make your own experimental verification of them. You will have the sense, happily, to make your trial runs in penny-ante games.

Other players are most likely to be driven out of a hand when you have the opportunity to bet heavily as the opener or directly following the opener. In other words, when you are the age or immediately left of the age, tactical conditions are thought optimum for playing a troublesome two pair or any such middling hand. It stands to reason that undecided players who follow you in the betting order—who are yet to "speak"—may be persuaded to sit this one out.

To build a pot it is most convenient to be nearly last to speak. Having already entered a pot, players are generally just a shade more reluctant to abandon it, or at least, not until the next card is dealt.

Try giving yourself a set of orders to follow. Play loose for an hour, tight for an hour, perhaps bluff once every hour on the hour. It makes no sense whatsoever to play poker this way, but you may find you can't follow your own instructions. I recommend the exercise for two reasons. First, it can enhance your sense of control of your own game, and second, more pragmatically, it can be necessary to play tight for an extended time. A few wins tend to cast a rosy glow over the game; players often react by throwing away chips on loose calls until at last a lower equilibrium is reestablished. Over and over again the early winner is bankrupt by the end of the evening; he couldn't hold on to what he made while the cards were running in his direction.

There is a reverse side to the problem of holding on to your winnings: a player with a sinking stake tends to choke his chances at some fair hands through mulish reluctance to bet. If you find you cannot play comfortably with the cushion remaining to you, leave the game instead of metering out the rest of your money in tentative dribbles. Or discipline yourself to play those last few opportunities to the hilt, even though you may break yourself faster. You will break yourself more surely in the desperate ordeal of trying to catch a sure thing with just a hoarded chip or two.

Play on nothing but hunches and intuition for a period. You must ascertain for yourself to what extent your feelings are to be trusted. Somewhere in the back of every poker player's mind is a nagging, suppressed wish to discover that winning is a simple matter of anticipating the cards.

9. methodology used in obtaining the odds

All tables for raw frequencies of hands (Tables 1, 2, and 12) were computed as straightforward combinations. Expectations on the draw (Tables 5, 6, 7, 8 11, 15, and 16) were, likewise, computed from combinations of the cards not visible. The method is unequivocal for five-card draw and hold 'em, but only an approximation for stud games. (Any improvement would entail an unwieldly number of contingency tables, describing each of a very large number of visible scenarios. Statistical inference as to the number of desirable cards remaining in the stock leads to high and low values, depending on the number of players remaining, stage by stage, in the game—an imponderable. Blind combinations lead to generally middling values between the extremes calculated in more specific ways. Thus, they are tolerably accurate as an expression of average expectations.)

Distributions of the hands in the showdown are also approximations, arrived at in the following ways:

Five-card draw We assume that players without four cards to a straight or flush or without at least a pair of nines (a figure based strictly on experience) fold in the opening round. Improved and unimproved hands are calculated on the basis of their expectations and retained or discarded according to the result (anything less than a pair of queens was discarded). The resulting compilation (Table 3) appears in the text.

Five-card stud This table (Table 9) arises out of a branched analysis carried forward with the average expectations on each draw. Unpaired openers or less than jack-high (another educated guess) were discarded outright. The complete, composite figures are sums of the branches in which no open pair, one open pair, two open pair, or visible trips appear, forcing the expected number of inferior hands out of play. No provision was made in five-card stud for the occurrence of straights and flushes because they are so rarely a part of an informed player's intentions.

Seven-card stud Frequencies of the hands (Table 13) were compiled from 1,000 eight-handed games, played in three degrees of randomly assigned conservatism: text-book openers; middling pairs and three-card flushes for two more cards; and any pair or three-card flush or straight (including high, inside straights) for two more cards after the opening. Within the limits of conservatism built into the data, and computing a sample standard error of proportion for each type of hand, the table thus obtained has a 99% degree of confidence with a maximum error of ±3% for most hands. (Two pair is ±4%; the three rarest hands—no pair, four of a kind, and straight flush—have a somewhat smaller, but less reliable, maximum error.) It is reasonable to assume, I think, that each type of hand would be distributed normally across a large number of thousand-game samples.

Tables for expectation of winning appear in the chapters on five-card draw (Table 4), five-card stud (Table 10), and seven-card stud (Table 14); the inappropriateness of such a table for hold 'em is explained in that chapter. The seven-card stud table (Table 14) arises out of the data. Those for the five-card games (Tables 4 and 10) are approximations derived from the showdown tables (Tables 3 and 9), assuming a binomial distribution. The method is acceptable in most instances in that the presence of any given hand at the table does not commonly reduce the occurrence of any other class of hand by more than 8%. (The obvious exception, of course, is two pair vs. trips, where the reduction in probability of trips is about 15%. However, since any error—and they are not large—leads to a slightly more conservative expectation of winning, no attempt has been made to refine the figures.) Any meaningful substitution of a hypergeometric for the binomial distribution in this problem would require that the frequency of each class of hand be defined in terms of every other hand; that is, how does a made flush affect the occurrence of a straight? two pair? and so forth. This is not a case of a simple "draw without replacement." The result would be a number of tables, none of which carry any real guarantee of greater accuracy, since the showdown tables are themselves approximations (as indeed they must always be).

The 25% figure, recommended in the chapter on seven-card stud as a significant ratio in drawing to straights and flushes, has the advantage of being easily calculated under game conditions. It is acceptably close to lengthier statistical inferences that might have been used in the same situations. The method is *not* recommended for gauging the odds after the fourth card and should be used *only* in decisions concerning straights and flushes.

10. glossary of common poker terms

age, edge The player immediately left of the dealer; his is the privilege of opening in draw poker.

ante A small, fixed amount placed in the pot by each participating player before the deal of a hand

back in To enter into the betting after having checked earlier in the round

beans Chips

bet A wager

bicycle In lowball, the lowest straight **A 2 3 4 5**

blind A bet placed before looking at one's cards; required in some poker variants

bluff Any attempt to represent a poker hand that the player does not hold

boat Full house

bull, bullet An ace

bump Raise

burn To take a card from the deck and out of play. Usually a burn card remains face down, but if it is shown to anyone it must be shown to all.

bust A hand containing not even a pair

buy-in A required minimum investment to enter the game. No player is required to stay in the game, merely to produce the buy-in amount when he joins the table.

call To meet a bet without increasing the amount

case card The fourth and last card of a rank to appear

check 1) To decline to bet when there are no previous bets in the round; 2) a poker chip

check and raise To first check and then raise any subsequent player who has initiated a bet

chicago A common dealer's choice variant of seven-card stud (rarely five-card stud) in which the high spade in the hole (concealed card) splits the pot; sometimes played with the low spade in the hole

cold deck A stacked deck

cowboy A king

dead man's hand Aces over eights, all black; said to have been the hand Wild Bill Hickok held when he was killed

deadwood Discarded and folded cards

dealer's choice Any poker session in which the dealer is required to designate the poker variant to be played in the hand he deals

deuce A two

down the river Seven-card stud

fever A five

fishhook A jack

flush Five cards all in the same suit

fold To throw one's cards in and quit a hand before the showdown

force-bet A required bet. Casino games often designate an opener and a minimum opening bet.

foul hand A hand that is not playable because of irregularity in the deal

free ride A betting round in which every active player has checked; thus nothing is owed the pot.

freeze-out Game in which, by agreement, no player may withdraw until he has either lost his entire stake or won all the others at the table

full house Three of a kind plus a pair

hole card In stud games, a concealed (face-down) card

hook A jack

inside straight A straight that lacks a card within its broken sequence. An outside straight, by contrast, is an unbroken sequence of four cards that lacks a fifth at either end of the sequence.

jacks or better In five-card draw, allowable openers not less than a pair of jacks

kick Raise

kicker An unpaired card; used to resolve ties in similar hands

knave A jack (British)

lady A queen

light A chip owed to the pot; it is drawn out of the pot and set aside by the borrower during play of a hand.

lock A sure thing

one pair Two cards of the same rank; also, the value of a hand that contains no more than one pair

openers Minimum value of a hand needed to begin the betting; no openers are required if none are specified either by the dealer or by the house rules.

open pair In stud games, a visible pair

pass and out; passout Game in which players are required to bet in the first round or leave play for the rest of the hand

pat hand A hand that cannot reasonably be improved by drawing cards

pot limit Game in which the maximum bet is fixed at the amount already in the pot

progressive poker If openers have been designated and the dealer has called for progressive openers, then the value of the required pair increases with each unopened hand. Thus, if no player could legally open in the first hand with a pair of jacks or better, the next hand will require a pair of queens at least. Generally, openers greater than a pair of aces are not specified.

raise To bet in excess of the amount required to call a bet

roll-your-own A brand of stud poker in which all cards are dealt face down and the usual number are turned face up in each round by each player

run A straight

sandbag To check and raise

showdown At the end of a game, when every active player has met his obligations to the pot, all surviving hands are shown face up, beginning with the last bettor or raiser and moving to the left, and compared to determine a winner.

shuck A card that may, on the player's option, be discarded and replaced

special hand An assortment of cards outside of the universally recognized poker hands that has value only by special prior agreement of the players

stakes 1) The rules that govern the size of bets at a table; 2) the relative scale of wagering in a game, as in high stakes or low stakes

straight An unbroken sequence of five cards

straight flush An unbroken five-card sequence all in the same suit

street In stud poker, term used to indicate a particular round: fifth street, for example, refers to that point in the game after the fifth card has been dealt to each player.

string bet An illegal method of making a bet in which a player adds chips to the pot in more than one installment. The bet must be made all in one motion.

ticket A card

trey A three

trips Three of a kind

under the gun Having a requirement to open or fold in the first round of a pass-and-out game

wheel In lowball, the smallest straight; see bicycle

wired pair In stud games, a pair dealt in the first two cards

11. suggestions for further reading

This list, a small fraction of the books about poker, is intended only to open the subject to a new enthusiast. Something of value can be learned from nearly any treatment of the subject, but I have included no purely "technical" nor psychologically labyrinthine approaches to the game.

Coffin, George S., *Fortune Poker*. Philadelphia: D. McKay Co., 1949. The author outlines most phases of the game and includes an exhaustive codification of the laws of poker.

Livingston, A. D., *Poker Strategy and Winning Play*. Hollywood: Wilshire, 1971. One of the ablest and most careful of writers on poker.

Morehead, Albert H., *The Complete Guide to Winning Poker*. New York: Simon and Schuster, 1967. Morehead's is a valuable introduction to the game of lowball.

Moss, John, *How to Win at Poker*. New York: Doubleday, 1973. This is a compact (92 pages) but extremely well thought out book by one of the game's most successful players.

Scarne, John, *Scarne on Cards*. New York: Crown, 1965. Scarne is an authority on the techniques and detection of cheating.

Yardley, Herbert O., *The Education of a Poker Player*. New York: Simon and Schuster, 1957. It's hard to classify Yardley's book; perhaps it's an instructional novel.